MEMORIES
of the
GREAT DEPRESSION
My Personal Memories

by

Jack Daniels

DORRANCE PUBLISHING CO., INC.
PITTSBURGH, PENNSYLVANIA 15222

ISBN # 0-8059-6442-8
Printed in the United States of America

First Printing

For information or to order additional books, please write:
Dorrance Publishing Co., Inc.
701 Smithfield Street
Third Floor
Pittsburgh, Pennsylvania 15222
U.S.A.
1-800-788-7654
Or visit our web site and on-line catalog at www.dorrancepublishing.com

To Karla

MEMORIES
of the
GREAT DEPRESSION

Peace + Love

Jack Daniels

04/04/04

This book is dedicated to those courageous nuns and priests of the Catholic faith who have honored their vows of celibacy and carry the cross of Jesus for all their sheep.

CONTENTS

ACKNOWLEDGMENTS

This book is written to honor my mother and father, who suffered in silence, hiding their grief in mortal souls; also my father, who always called me "Jack," as have my many dear friends. Thus my pen name "Jack Daniels."

And to my lovely wife, who shares in my salvation from those memories with kindness and peace.

FORWARD

This is a true story of my life during the Great Depression. As I recall, life was hard for most in many ways. Wealth was usually a protectant from cruel and/or unjust treatment. Those others who survived were honed sharp for future life. They served their country in its greatest time of need.

There were two kinds of depression—one, a lack of available jobs; and two, depression in mind and spirit. Into that chaos my family and I ground out an existence and survived; how is now told.

As a child born in 1924, I grew into an eighteen-year-old adult ready for military service in World War II. The story is one of struggle and choices families made to survive and eke out some pleasures regardless of being obliged to live on the edge year to year.

Jack Daniels
April 15, 2002

INTRODUCTION

This book reveals what occurred at a particular point in time. My experiences are burned into my psyche, as are those of my father, mother, sisters, and all the others who moved through my life. Please enjoy history, for each one's is unique.

Writing this book concerns individual events as they unfolded during my early years from birth to eighteen. The lack of wealth certainly played a definitive role in all the events as they occurred. We were fortunate to survive as well as we did, and now I thank God for providing the many experiences for they were rare, amusing, and educational. Our families finally did all right. The war provided me with the growth and maturity necessary at just the right time; it was my childhood dream to be a soldier and so it became real. What more can anyone hope for, a dream, wish, desire fulfilled.

My Catholic education did not end in grade school. Although high school was not parochial, it was another great event in my life. I was propelled from a very regimented environment into a structured education system allowing one to progress through different instructors skilled in several subjects. Also, the change in students during the day allowed for more social growth. The students were also from different cultures, races, and religions with ethnic backgrounds, which fashioned new conversations and knowledge. I was truly happy.

My college education after the war was in schools affiliated with religious institutions. There were lay teachers and religious teachers who were available for certain subjects. Those orders made sure that the students were well qualified in their chosen studies. A Catholic education provided in the 1920s and 1930s was far different, depending on the nuns and priests to do all the educating.

CHAPTER 1:

1924: Mound Street, Birth to Two—Oh Birth, Oh Bugs

I, a Depression person born in 1924, have contemplated the Great Depression as it affected my life in an average American family. The reason I do this is to keep alive what happens to people trapped in the throes of the collapse of financial institutions, and the resulting effect on ordinary families.

Memories of the Great Depression usually were devastating, however some of those events not only enlightened but they separated men and women from boys and girls. Certainly the young men and women who lived during the period prior to the start of World War II, who suffered during that Depression, had weathered the loss of a normal existence; struggled through the despair evident in a society with masses of jobless and families living on the edge for the basic necessities of life; and were of an age just ripe for military service. To those young men and women who had weathered the storm of Depression, the military offered a new life, the opportunity to serve God and Country, and all the resplendent benefits of serving their country.

Many American citizens were not affected by the Great Depression as my family was—no, there were the fortunate. Those in state, federal, county, and city jobs could provide for their families. Those on farms had food at least, and the wealthy who survived the stock market crash were, for the most part, unaffected. My family was not included. We were a family caught in the maelstrom. My family survived but each of us was victim of others who either were ignorant of those suffering or had hardened their hearts.

Into this atmosphere I appeared on the screen of life. How was I to react to the many diverse, disappointing, exciting, entertaining, and completely awesome places, persons, and events evident in 1924 with the Great Depression coming in a few years?

1

How can anyone know what another person has really experienced. How in their wildest imagination can that be possible? It is not! So we are then content to leave ourselves open to the scrutiny of the great ones, the educated, the experienced—oh give me a laxative. Yuk. So now in older age, contemplation becomes a clear road to reconciling fact and fiction, lies and truth, dreaded thoughts and reality. With age comes the cooling of temper, the search for mental justice, and the final tussle with one's own spirit.

Thinking back to the beginning is easy. Where it all happened is a little cloudy for the first few years, but one can imagine based on later experience how it all was in those days, the molding of a person, the individual response to the design of others, the very essence of being a human being all wrapped up in smells, feels, and sounds. Yes, going back is possible, so let us begin.

Dad said, "This house has bugs—bed bugs." We were in a rental flat. You know, those two- or three-story flats lined up on a tree-lined street. We were on the first floor and I was somewhere in the neighborhood of two to three—not important. The important part, according to Dad, was BUGS. The sight of Dad and Mom scurrying around taking the bedding, mattresses, and rugs outside and spraying some foul-smelling liquid was mind-boggling. My older sisters were talking about what if the neighbors saw or heard or knew, but at that point it seemed Dad did not care, nor did Mom. Bugs ruled the day. I remember long conversations on what kind of dirty, rotten person had previously lived in this flat. This is a definite memory I will never forget. The smell of solvent, especially Lysol, permeated the air for days. My four- and seven-year-old sisters were nauseated.

Another vivid memory is of my sisters looking out the window at night. They were looking at a young lad sitting on his bed in the flat next door. I heard them talking and acting like they were throwing up and then laughing and calling for Mom. What they saw was the young lad eating the stuff between his toes, which they called toe jam. Now that never left my memory and to this day every time I wash my feet, that memory lingers on.

The Catholic Church was just through the backyard across the street. It, the priests' house, and the sisters' residence occupied the whole block. I was made aware of the fact that I had been baptized there—yes, I had bellowed so loud the priest made many remarks about a big mouth, lungs, etc., and he hoped I would be as vocal about the church as I was in yelling at him.

My sisters were of school age and for the year and a half we lived there, they were occupied with school. However during summer recess they would be in charge of yours truly. One fine day they put me in a small buggy and pushed the buggy up and down the street, faster and faster. My recollection is of exhilaration until the buggy hit the end of the sidewalk and down I and it went, over and over into the street. Shouting, screaming, and blood on my face is what I remember. Mom came running, and of course that was the end of the fun of riding the buggy. I felt sorry for my sisters, especially since Mom had her way with bottom treatments.

The folks had good friends just one block away who owned their own home. Their backyard was a forest of bushes and a large grape arbor. We kids would go over to their house and play back in their bushes and the grape arbor. Summertime was so good, with the warm sun, the blue sky, and the smells of plants, grass, and laundry on the clothes lines. Those too became play-grounds, us kids running between the laundry and hiding behind the sheets. That home had long clothes lines and playing between the clothes lines and also the bushes and arbor filled many a day in the summer. Our rental had a lousy backyard, just flat to the street behind, so we spent many days at the folks' friends' house. They had a boy and a girl. The boy was not friendly too me—perhaps it was because I was just going on three—but the girls got along fine. Mom and her friend would sit and watch us play on those wonderful summer days. When the grapes came in both families enjoyed grape jam, which the two moms made and shared. Now I can realize the value of own-ing your own home. One thing I remember for sure was that those friends had a rule in their home—only flush the toilet once a day. Dad used to laugh about that and say, "What a mess that must be at the end of day." Dad was a plumber and had better vision. His vision of toilets, bathrooms, stinks, and slim, I knew, conjured up a nightmare scenario of grotesque proportions. Enough said. Need I clarify a plumbers life? Then there is this tale he told me years later. Dad was working in the basement of a funeral home. The morti-cian evidently forgot he was unplugging a trap to the basement. The trap was an overhead affair and as Dad progressed on the job, with the trap open, the mortician released fluids from a corpse he was working on. Down onto poor Dad it poured. Oh, for the life of a plumber in the 1920s!

Mother was fixated on being a super-Catholic Christian. She had a sis-ter who was a nun and a sister who worked for the government. Her other three sisters were from a second marriage. My grandfather had died when my mother was three years old, which was difficult. Mom was sent to a nun-nery when she was thirteen, but she did not stay. I heard tales of her tor-ment in making a final decision to leave and go home. Now I consider that a mighty brave step for a young girl to make just after the turn of the cen-tury, but she was free-willed about some things yet a real heller when it came to "do as I say." One thing she objected to at the nunnery was taking a bath with a robe on so as not show the body. That was too much. She had been through enough. Grandfather had died, Grandmother was pregnant with Mom's sister, and Mom had been through burdensome times after that. They moved back to Wisconsin from Minnesota and came home to the grandparents. Some time later Grandmother married again.

My memory of church in those days was hearing many sermons on hell and damnation. What I concluded was that sin must be in every nook, cranny, corner, and element of society. Everyone is afflicted with this sin disease, including the rich but especially the poor. Whatever. Now there was no definition of race involved. Everyone was included, so beware, it is everywhere. Those years 1924 through 1928 were good years. They were so good Dad and Mom bought a home. I remember talk of moving not too far away to a real nice neighborhood and the home was new.

The whole event of moving was completed in no time. We did not have that much furniture, just enough. The home was small yet was just comfy for a family of five with just enough room. It was summer and just wonderful because we had open land behind and a beautiful street.

Now as I contemplate on moving and adjusting to everything, including neighbors, streets, houses, and distances, it all becomes more significant as it affects the human psyche. This move, the first in my life, was just the beginning in the tragedy inflicted on children and their parents in a world gone wild. During the next sixteen years my family was destined to move eight times. Does that sound plausible, tragic, horrid, and disturbing? Yes, it was, and all a part of the Great Depression. As a survivor, now seventy-eight years old, I can tell you without equivocation that to live through those years was a living hell, but we did not know it. We were aware of it, but like melted iron we cooled with time into humans with hardened personalities.

We always went to Grandmother's home, which was in the central part of town, close to downtown and stores of all kinds with movie theaters and all the excitement that they bring. Thanksgiving, Christmas, and birthdays were very often spent in those fun visits. Since we did not have a car, the street car was our chariot to the other world.

CHAPTER 2:

1926: Wingra Street, Two to Five—Oh Joy, Oh Sorrow

My recollection of that first house, where I grew from two to five is remarkable since I can remember so many instances of joy and excitement. The time was between 1926 and 1928. Our house was small but warm. My sisters were in the same grade school; Mary was six and Cres was eleven. All summer long it was great, walking in the park and zoo near our home with Mom. We had a great garden and a street that had little traffic since it dead-ended at a fountain. When the girls were in school, Mom and I would have lazy times walking around the neighborhood and going to the store at the corner. We used to take the street car downtown, about three miles away, since we had no car. One time on that street car Mom was talking to a friend about me, saying all those juicy, braggy things moms say about children. Suddenly she asked me to turn around so her friend could really see the joy of her life. I was a row ahead and across from Mom, and for some reason a dark and sinister thing stirred in my head, so as I turned I stuck out my tongue. Boy, the reaction was like a dynamite explosion. Talk about a *look*—it would freeze an Eskimo instantly! The trip was a disaster and when I got home, what a walloping I got. Never disgrace your mother.

When we lived there we had one of those winters when it snows sixty-plus inches. The neighborhood kids dug tunnels in the empty lot next to our house; talk about fun crawling, for hours it seemed, through the tunnels. At four years I could stand up in the main igloo entrance. I always wondered what would have happened if it had collapsed on us.

One other exciting experience, really exciting, occurring during these years was when we were shucking corn on the back porch. It was a beautiful day, warm, with the overwhelming smell of corn and cut grass. The air was calm, Mom was humming some new songs, and I was trying to keep up.

5

Suddenly we heard horrible, loud, blood-curdling noises from the zoo. One could only imagine gore, blood, and even death. Death it was. We ran through the garden and field to the zoo road. The noise had stopped but shouting men could be heard. Mom said, "Just stay here." In a short time a person came and said a male bear had killed a young bear. Images of that stayed imbedded in my young mind for years.

Dad had worked as an iceman for the local ice company. There was a huge cement building situated about a block from one of our lakes. In the winter the company's men ventured out on the ice and cut blocks of ice, then moved them to the icehouse and stored them for the summer. There was no refrigeration as we have nowadays. It was arduous work and extremely dangerous. Dad also delivered the ice from the ice truck pulled by the gallant horses. With the plumbing industry in depression, the ice wagons still came.

What fun it was for us kids. We would run to the back of the ice wagon and search for broken shards of ice. Sometimes, if the iceman was kind, he would give out the pieces. We had cards in the house on which were printed the numbers 100, 75, 50, and 25. You turned the card to show in a window with the amount you desired on top. We usually went with fifty pounds. The iceman, with his prong, picked up the ice block, brought it into the house, put it in the refrigerator's top drawer, and that was that. This was simple and effective for a few days, but hard work. The blocks were cut into 100 pound blocks, so lifting and cutting for the iceman was brutal work. Dad's strength was improved for his eventual work as a plumber, since in those days the tubs were solid iron, as were sinks for kitchens and baths. They were also covered with porcelain, all extremely heavy.

I had an unfortunate incident just before we left the house near the zoo. The neighbor boys—there were two older than I—wanted to play hide and seek. I had not played with them much before because they were usually gone with their folks, who owned a large food and meat market near my grandmother's. This particular day they were home and so asked me to play. I hid behind the thick bush in front of the house next to ours. Their home was brick, located just down the street. I saw the boy who was "it" looking for one of us out hiding. He caught his brother and that left me. All of a sudden the brother came around the side of the house behind me and let me know he found me. His brother came running and entered the bushes with a rock in his hand and slammed it on my head twice. It was painful and caused me to howl and run home with blood on my hand from the wound. My mother cleaned the wound, but since they had money it was forgotten. Mother was cowed by people with wealth.

However, disaster struck when Dad's plumbing job started to go sour. The Depression of 1929 was wreaking havoc on construction. Dad's employer was non-union and that did not help the situation. Steady income disappeared, loan payments added up, and we were forced to move from our comfortable home and pleasant surroundings. Grandmother gave notice that there was a rental up the block, so Dad made a decision and we moved to a two-flat, first floor, on a street called Doty.

We really did not have much to move. Luckily it was summer and with help from Dad's shop we were moved. Mother had been fortunate to have been given an older piano from Grandmother. She played beautifully, and my sisters would spend much time singing and learning to play under Mother's tutoring. My dad was also an excellent tenor singer. I loved to hear them sing, although my own young attempts lent little to their songs. So we arrived at our new uptown location.

The house was old, but no one lived upstairs, so that was good. I was informed that school was on the horizon, about two months away. The first friends I met at that location were Catholics like my family. They all attended the Catholic Church and school just one block away. Thus began a traumatic adjustment for young me. My mother's family was ensconced in the older German school and church seven blocks away. None of my friends went there.

Just a side note on that school—Mother's grandfather had provided the church with the main altar, a large edifice in those days. He also provided the land for the sisters' house and the house itself. My mother's sister was a nun in the Notre Dame order with close affiliations with that school. This was all stacked against me. Consequently, my two sisters and I had no out, and we were enrolled. Living near downtown was a monumental change in many respects.

Uptown meant being close to all those exciting things like stores, theaters, and restaurants, yet it was disappointing since they all required money, which we kids did not have. Dad, out of work, depended on part-time jobs based on his reputation as a first-class plumber. Those contacts were few and far between. The rent had to be paid, along with buying the very necessities of life—food, utilities, and school. With Grandma and Granddad just down the street, Mom found some money in the way of doing cleaning, laundry, and some cooking for her sisters and stepsisters. They were in their twenties and thirties, working for various businesses, and they were more than willing to have Mom perform those duties.

Shortly after our arrival, a local grocery where Mom shopped needed part-time help. Mom applied and was hired, her small income greatly appreciated. So we were surviving.

Next door was a beautiful three-flat made of brick and ornate stone, which further made our rental look like an old relic. Kids are aware of these sorts of things. On the second floor lived a great kid named Billy. Billy and I were the same age and became great friends. His folks had money and even at my age of five they impressed me. You see, my folks talked about money a lot. They discussed people and homes and places that all spelled money. I heard a lot of this and had it in my mind that things like homes, food, clothes, and transportation like cars, carriages, etc., meant money. Anyway, Billy came from money, and we became good friends. He, however, went to the school one block away, which for me meant disaster, since with school coming soon it meant separation.

Our move had occurred in May and that meant play time outside. Billy and I dug up that barren backyard playing all sorts of games which required digging trenches for make-believe armies and enemies and friends. There were three garages in one building along the back lot line. One was empty so we used that as a playhouse. My sisters would chase us and it seemed like forever since when they caught us it was endless tickling. Tickling is delicious fun for the tickler but for me it was torment to the edge of sanity. I still can feel that helpless feeling. They were now eight and twelve, just the right age to hold me down.

Billy was interested in smoking. He had not tried it but he talked about it and described how his dad and mom seemed to love smoking cigarettes. Billy told me that when visiting the grocery store where my mother worked he saw the glass cigarette case at the front of the store. The conversation for five-year-olds ran from "How do we obtain cigarettes" to "How do we obtain those particular cigarettes." Billy was more graphic in his ideas than I; he subscribed to my getting them from my mother or even better me taking them. Well guess what? I was weak, weak enough to agree that I, at five, should do the dastardly deed.

The next day we walked down to the grocery store. He looked in and said, "Your mom is in the back of the store. Just do it." I crawled in the front door, around the edge of the case, and grabbed a pack, then crawled back out and we ran home.

We stood behind one of those garage doors and discussed our next illicit act. Billy agreed to grab matches from his mother's dresser. Soon we had everything we needed. We opened the pack like Billy had seen his folks do. They smelled all right. Billy suggested we go down to the lake where my sisters and his mother would not discover us. Great. Although we were not allowed to go the three blocks to the lake, we did. The trip went fast in anticipation of that first smoke. The pier at the one beach that was available for our neighborhood seemed to stretch forever. We went to the very end, opened the pack, each put a cigarette in our mouth, lit the match, lit the end, and drew in those supposedly delicious breaths of tobacco. I took two large draws and blew the blue smoke out, then another and another, and then came the feeling of the sky moving strangely, the nausea, and the heaving over the end of the pier. My world was ending, it seemed; I prayed, *God, please let me feel better now.* Billy was in the same boat, gagging and spitting, and then he threw up. After a period with both of us miserably sick, ashamed, afraid, and disgusted with smoking, we threw the pack in the water and walked home. It was a long, long time before we ever smoked again. The cigarettes were called Fatima.

My dad was a great cigar smoker. He did not inhale them but he enjoyed them. Every room smelled of that cigar smoke. Dad always bought the cheapest but it made no difference—it seemed like he did more sucking than smoking. The butt was always wet and he held it in his mouth a long time after no smoke was present. Dad, in those days, was in his early thirties. He also enjoyed a good shot of whiskey, and that was also always the cheapest he could get. Whiskey was rarely seen in our home since money was used for food first.

The summer went by. We spent some time at the beach, my sisters, my friend Billy, and I. It was great learning to swim and playing in the sand. The water was so clean you could see the bottom of the lake at least fifty yards out. In later years, we enjoyed the lake even more.

But the summer went fast, and school became a word often used with extra emphasis on *school, conduct, nuns,* and *priests,* all to be revered. Too much of that was really too scary for a now six-year-old. You see, my birthday was in June (Gemini) and that meant I left school usually on my birthday. So school days began the first week in September for my sisters and me.

First grade for me, with my sisters in fifth and seventh respectively, was at the Catholic school with Notre Dame nuns. We were poor so our clothes were usually found at the used goods stores. I believe Mother used stores like we have nowadays, like Goodwill or the Salvation Army. I did not know what they were but I knew that was where the clothes came from. So that September day, the three of us walked the seven blocks to school, a trip repeated by each of us until each left the eighth grade. What a journey through adolescence.

Well, I was scared shitless. Yes, we arrived and were lined up by class in the hall and marched into our respective rooms. The seats were wood— oak—and Sister warned of writing on, scratching, or in any way harming the tops. I noticed all sorts of marks and letters on the one assigned to me. Oh, well. I was last in the first row, since we were assigned seats by height— tall in the back, short in the front; girls in a row, then boys, about forty-five students total.

CHAPTER 3:

1929: Doty Street, Five to Seven—Oh School

The first day of school at age six nowadays is more of a joy. Preparation begins for most kids in preschool, with induction sessions for parents and children, TV education, and all the government intervention in school. Back then fear of failure and teachers, especially for poor children, was just a big social problem. Rich families were always up front. Even though Great-grandfather had done much for the church, he was long gone, and our family gleaned no social status from our present condition. We were considered poor, poor, very poor.

The nuns were revered in those days. I was used to nuns due to my family's relatives, who were nuns. Our first grade teacher was pleasant but strict. You went to the bathroom at noon and that was that. However, my most distinct memory of that first day in school was not being allowed to go to the bathroom when I really needed to go. I asked and was refused that afternoon. School had started at eight sharp; every day of the school year we marched to church at that time and attended mass, then went back to the classroom. You could not speak in mass—do not turn your head, and do not fidget. My problem was that I needed to have a bowel movement, and even though I asked twice it was no. Eventually my bowels let loose in the afternoon, just about twenty minutes before we were released at four. That event tortured me for years. My mother said nothing, because you could never criticize a nun, even though Mom's experience as a novitiate nun was a disaster. She told us how they had to take a bath with their bodies covered with a gown and also how her friend crawled out a window and left the nun's dormitory. Mom, I believe, was traumatized by her experience. She loved the nuns and would back their teaching job, but being a nun was not for her.

The rule of the ruler was evident during that first grade. You sat straight, you held your pencil or pen properly, you did not talk unless asked to, and you came and went at the pleasure of the nun. That first year was a lifetime learning experience.

To digress a bit, the school was made of large gray blocks of granite with the largest areas covered by gray brick. The entrance was foreboding in appearance, with steep cement steps, at least twelve, and heavy sidewalls just high enough for a six-year-old to peer over and heavy steel black banisters. The actual opening into the school yawned with heavy cement columns, as was the arched entrance, at least twelve feet high, which led back to the doors about eight feet away. The halls, one on each floor, were long with extra high ceilings, lit by hanging lights. Both floors were identical. The schoolrooms were aligned along the hall with an end room on each floor. The first floor included the first through fourth grades, with the nurse station at the end of the hall. The second floor included the fifth through eighth grades, with the principal's office at the far end. Both floors had boys' and girls' restrooms. There was a very wide front staircase on both sides of the entrance. That entrance area was fairly large, the staircases were wide, and the ceiling went clear to the roof. The back staircase was very narrow, with a similar ceiling, high, dark, and gloomy. Both staircases had banisters. All in all, the school was gloomy, dark, and to put it bluntly, not inviting. Into that environment I, at age six that summer of 1930, was thrust with my two beautiful sisters.

Since we were a God-fearing, baptized, poor, humble family, Mother bore the brunt of getting us ready for the new school. My dad was busy just making ends meet by still doing odd jobs in his trade of plumbing. Dad was a gentle, kind, and quiet soul. My Mom's sister, the nun, had been a visitor in the summer and extolled on the virtues of the school we would be attending. She knew the school but was not familiar with all the nuns who were assigned there. My sisters were well prepared from their former encounter in the previous Catholic school and feared not, while I was not prepared for that type of regimentation. You could call it discrimination, but since we were all white and of European extraction, who cared—poor were poor and rich were rich and it just was like that.

I did learn the basics in the environment. There was no out—you either learned or else and for my future life, which became fifty percent military, the rule of order was best. During that time we had visits at Grandmother's house down the street with our relatives who were nuns. Mom always warned us to be on our best conduct and answer questions with positive answers. To a six-year-old waiting for seven, that was the right thing, for being anything but correct meant Mom's wrath later. Both of those nuns were always pleasant and actually fun to be around. One was a principal of a high school and the other of a grade school. I always enjoyed seeing and hearing them talk about their work, and I had no problem answering their questions. We always had great dinners at Grandmother's house with plenty of sweets. My sisters were so kind and gentle, everyone loved them. Mom was always proud of them.

One day we received a gift. One of my aunts from Grandmother's house gave my mom our first radio. It was a cabinet-type model, not new, but the first one I remember. That evening we all sat or laid in front of the radio. That radio was on all the time and became Mom's daily home companion, and as time went on she had her favorite daily programs. I remember one called "Mother Monohan" was special.

Christmas came that year with all attention on church and Christian duties. Dad was not bringing in much money, so he and I went looking for a tree that we found for twenty-five cents. It was just a few days before Christmas and when we got it home, Mom cried. It was not much more than a small bush about four feet high with sparse limbs and not that many needles, but we put it up. We kids did not expect much and that was the way it was.

The big event was Christmas dinner at Grandmother's. Mom and Aunt Helene played their piano and we all sang Christmas songs while waiting for supper, after which we played games.

Winter in Wisconsin always had lots of snow and cold. Our house was cold. Coal was expensive and it seemed we heard much conversation on coal, money, and rent. That winter, luckily, was not as cold so we spent more time playing in the snow. Billy was happy with his school, which according to him was fun, games, and very liberal. I envied Billy and his school, one block away, and all bright and shining. He had received a great train for Christmas, which I really wondered over because it was so beautiful and must have cost a fortune. We only got together on weekends since it was dark out early in winter and school studies took up each evening.

When spring arrived our first grade teacher talked to the boys in the class about becoming servers for the priests. We had two priests, one an assistant learning how to run a parish. Usually they stayed about two to three years. They both required servers at each mass. There were normally two masses a day which required servers, however, there were special occasions like daily masses for the nuns in their quarters early in the morning, which would require a child to be there at 6 A.M. The training for this privilege was during first and second grade. I had no way out, since most Catholic mothers expected their sons to become priests. I could not figure why I never heard her expecting the girls to become nuns. Was it due to her experiences?

We boys were trained to say prayers in Latin, and the Confiteor was most difficult for servers. Over and over and over we recited the prayers after school. We provided the answer to the priest's prayer. My sisters were required to wait for me. They were very patient, God bless them.

During the next spring my friend Billy and some of his friends from school went down to the beach and went swimming. Thaw had opened the lake early, and spring was unusually warm, which saved coal, too. I saw Billy that weekend but then learned he was ill, very ill.

It went on like that for two weeks, then we found out Billy had a serious disease called meningitis. They figured it was the result of swimming in too-cold water and the resulting chills and fever. Nowadays they would have more information on the cause. His death in the third week hurt me as only a six-year-old can be. He was my good and only close friend, since I had no friends living close by. They were all over the hill on the way to school, and if they lived on the hill they were wealthy and so identified by the school. Mom and Dad helped me get over the effect with tender loving care.

The warming weather brightened my life somewhat. Dad had me help him with our strange bathroom tub. Over the tub was a big gas heater, which was the water heater for baths. It really was mounted so one end was over the end of the tub where the cold water faucet was. To take a bath you lit the gas heater inside the bottom side with a taper, then waited until the water was hot. You could tell that by feeling the side since the water heated up. Then you mixed the hot and cold water to the proper feel. I watched him fix the heater, handing him the tools, then he fixed the cold water faucet since it leaked. That was the first time I really felt I was helping. Dad was filling my mind with other thoughts.

However other events started very soon, for we were forced to move. Although Dad paid the rent, the owner decided to move back to the house. So there we were, forced to move again. Dad found a home at the other end of the block, a two-story flat, and the same situation was present—we would be the only occupants. As soon as school was out we would move. Well, that was something, so the rest of my stay in school went fast, I passed the first grade, I was reading some books, I was preparing to be a mass server, and I was moving again—wasn't that exciting? Moving on to second grade, I wondered if since religious education was always a priority part of our school education, would we be told more stories like we heard in first grade that horrified us kids? Like the ones the nun told us about the rabbi who entered a synagogue with sin on his soul. Upon leaving he was struck dead and his belly burst open and worms poured out. Or the one about black people who were black because they were descendants of Cain, who had slain Abel. Talk about fear and feeling like puking at the rabbi story! Us kids felt that way.

It all made me worry about what she had said so I asked Mom. I could tell by her face she was shocked. She was silent a bit and then said, "Well you know black and white are basic colors and everything in between is just part of their beauty, right?"

"Well I guess so," I replied. "But what about the rabbi?"

"The rabbi is Jesus for priests and they can be sinful like anyone else."

"But what about the worms?" I could tell she was getting a little frustrated.

"Well, you certainly love fishing with Dad and aren't worms his favorite bait?"

That sort of put it in a different realm. I thought, *Then why didn't the nun tell it that way so we would not be so scared? Oh well.*

CHAPTER 4:

1931: South Broom, Seven to Eight—Oh Summer Freedom

The school year ended with somber warnings that second grade would be harder, requiring more study and more training to be servers. Well, warm weather, turning seven on almost the last day of school, and the house move all made my summer a bright one.

My sisters and I went down and looked over the flat on Broom Street. Not bad; a little newer, no one on the second floor again, and it was right behind Grandmother's house—great! My future was looking brighter. Dad had some friends help us with the move. Everything went, including the piano. I was still too young to really help but I did my best carrying small things down the street to the new location. Since the weather was warm it made it all the better, because the lake was just down the block from this home. You could actually see it from the front porch.

We got settled in. In the fall my two sisters would enter the fifth and freshman years and did many chores around the house. It was quite a change living next to Grandmother's house. She was fond of flowers and had an area full of bleeding hearts, which I grew to love. They were so prolific. Adults occupied the flat next door with one child, a girl. It was a very short block, and across the street were two homes. One was very small but well kept, and it was in that home I found my new friend, and what a friend he was. If ever there were a Huckleberry Finn, it was in the likes of Sunny. I was sitting on the front steps, which were very high, with many steps to our flat watching Sunny, I called to him, lying on his front porch. He was nine, two years older than I was. He walked over to where I sat, and we became friends pretty fast. His dad was a switchman for the railroad, my dad a plumber. They owned their house, we rented; he had no brothers or sisters, I had sisters. It was easy to be friends. One thing he really interested me in was fishing. He knew all

15

about the best places on the lake to shore fish, just a hop, skip, and jump from my front porch. Great. I told him my dad would fix me up with what gear I would need, and we could plan some fishing days. I was greatly excited.

That summer of 1931 was a joy. Oh, it had its scary moments, but all in all, even with the Depression, young as I was, there were blue skies, a new good friend, and time off for fun.

Dad fixed me up with fishing gear—a short cane pole, line, and hooks—and a can to hold my worms. He and I would gather those critters together.

My mother still worked at the store and at Grandmother's. She was busy and I at seven had a lot of free rein. As I look back and contemplate on freedom, my children were not so lucky. Changing times and morals made it more difficult to allow tomboy and girl excursions than back then. What a joy it was, freedom to roam, to explore, just to be trusted. Mom always warned what would be the outcome of insubordinate behavior, and at that young age I respected Mom's and Dad's commandments as I did the Ten Commandments. There were gray areas in minding, but crossing the line was a no-no.

Mother was under strain. She had lost two children to the early 1920 epidemic of whooping cough and influenza. One was a boy and one was a girl. Both of them died very early in their life, but she did not reveal any more. The many moves, the Depression, and the worry over money wore her down. Shortly after we moved in, I was standing on the sidewalk in front of the house when she was walking back from Grandmother's house and just fell flat on the sidewalk. I ran to her and found no response. She was completely unconscious. Fortunately a man driving by in one of those electric cars stopped and after fanning her face, received some response. He asked me where we lived. I told him, "Right here," so he picked her up and with some difficulty carried her up the stairs and into the house. I showed him the bedroom and he asked who he could call, so I said, "Please tell my grandmother next door." He very graciously did that and Grandmother came over and administered to Mom.

The doctor came and said that Mom was physically exhausted and required complete rest for at least a week. Luckily it was summer, so the girls were readily available to do the housework. I was told to just stay out of trouble. Dad had been limping about for a week, then it became so bad he was obliged to see a doctor. He had stepped on a rusty nail while working at an old house part-time for a contractor. The foot had swelled and he was told to stay home and soak the foot in a solution of boric acid daily. This he did for a week, and thank the Lord, the poison came out—no big problem, since the real worry was a tetanus infection. Gradually Mom and Dad improved, to the joy of the girls, since their chores prevented any chance to get out and enjoy the weather.

During this time my friend and I became really close. Sunny seemed to always have change in his pocket which he gladly shared with me by buying treats at the grocery store. I would see quarters, dimes, and nickels in his hand every day it seemed. I knew his dad had steady work on the railroad, so maybe he was given money. Well, no such thing. One day he had no money, so he said, "Why don't you go and get some from your mom." I told him I didn't think she had any. He said, "Just go in and see if any is lying around." I never saw this in our house and had no reason to ever ask for some money. Sunny then revealed to me that he always saw money in their house on tables and bureaus and he just took what he wanted. Gosh, what a revelation! One thing I knew from my parents was we had no money to waste, lose, or have stolen. As it was, I still had bad dreams about the fact that I had really stolen a pack of cigarettes, which I regretted.

It did not change my feeling for him, it just made me feel he had a problem. Anyway, we decided to go fishing. I told Dad I needed worms. That night when it was really dark, he and I took his flashlight to Grandmother's lawn and hunted worms, and slimy, slippery things they are. That night I learned the art of catching night crawlers. Also, I learned the sexual niceties of catching these worms, two for one pounce. Dad had the technique—lay your hand softly on the worm or worms, just hard enough to hold, then with the other hand use your fingers to pull it slowly from the hole.

The next morning Sunny and I walked down to the lake. At that time the pier was there but the beach had not been completed, so swimming was not allowed like it was when the city really cleared out the area and made a really nice beach. We did not use the pier since there usually were men using it early in the morning.

At that time there was a large area between the railroad tracks that ran along behind the houses and school that looked out over the lake and the tracks that ran close to the lake. That area was all grass and a great play area. From the end of our street we turned right and walked along the tracks to one of two wooden bridges on the tracks that ran along the lake. Sunny had fished there before, and he was well aware of the risk using the bridge to fish from, however we could crawl down between the tracks and fish off the supports. There we could fish in deep water and be safe as the train came. This we did. We shared the worms, threaded them onto the hooks and started fishing. Actually in those days you could see the fish swimming around the pilings.

With the sun shining bright in the summer sky, a very warm day with a nice lake breeze and fishing, it was perfect. God was so good. But the fish did not bite. Try as we could, the fish did not bite. But it was still fun. Sunny heard it first—the rumbling of a train. He said, "Now just sit still. Do not stand up, and do not panic. Hold your head down and close your eyes 'cause the train has lots of things that fly off." Closer and closer it came, loud, rumbling, roaring, clanking—God, this was something. That first time was absolutely breathtaking. It was awesome, glorious, scary, and a lifetime experience never to be forgotten. It happened many more times, but at seven it was exhilarating. I will never forget looking up at the engine and every car go by. I thought, *Why would a fish bite with that frightening noise.* Sunny said, "No they are used to it." Well, no fish, so we started back and hunted along the huge rocks that rimmed the lake, which had been dumped years before to hold the shore because of the tracks.

Our journey was really rewarding. First we found dead fish, big old carp and garpike. Carp were prolific in that lake. One time they netted boxcars full of carp and sent them east to fisheries. That had been about five years before, according to Sunny. The garpikes were nasty looking, with big snouts full of teeth. We decided to put some of each on the tracks and watch the next train squish them. Sunny said it wouldn't be long, and it wasn't. We put some longwise on the track and some across. Soon the train came and what a sight— fish parts all over. Never had I been more elated! Sunny was a genius in my mind. It was great.

We finally tired of just hunting around the rocks and the smell of other fish that were rotting along the rocks. What an adventure for me at seven years old. I'll never forget that first day, followed by many more. You know, in those days our folks did not worry about us, life was good, if poor; life was clean; and people were kind, at least in our town at that time. We finally got home tired and ready to start a new adventure.

My dad was concerned we caught no fish because they would be another meal for the family. I did bring back the unused worms, so Dad said he and I would go that night. I was elated. After supper, with the girls in control at home, we traveled back to the lake. Dad had a long bamboo fishing pole. He fitted me out with a medium-sized one and away we went just as the sun was setting. We walked down to the lake with Dad whistling all the time. He really whistled beautifully. He had some favorite rocks to fish off of. They were not occupied by anyone else so we fixed our worms on the hooks and sent them out for fish. Dad had a bite within fifteen minutes, a big largemouth bass, about a two pounder. He had brought a pail, which he used for the fish after adding the lake water. Pretty soon he had another bite, a bullhead, a real nice one of about two pounds. Then I had a bite. He said, "Let it take it," as the cork bobbed up and down. Since this would be my first fish, he came over to help. We watched the cork start to travel and he said, "Lift the end of the pole fast," which I did. To my surprise I could feel the weight of the fish as it traveled around on the hook.

That fish went left, right, back, and forth, tugging until I figured it must be attached to the bottom. Dad saw my difficulty, put his pole down, and assisted me with the catch. Well, I had me a turtle—a big, bad-looking snapper. Rotten luck. We hauled it in, and although we had no scale, Dad estimated the weight at around three pounds. He said, "This is a typical large lake snapping turtle." I had never seen such a big turtle. Evidently I had my hook too low, since turtles love to bottom feed and a big, juicy night crawler was its dessert. Carp also are bottom feeders, scooping up the gunk one finds on the lake floor. That was what I thought we had on the hook. Dad used his pliers, and with me holding the back of the turtle down, snapped the hook from the turtle's lip. Back it went into the water. We caught three more bullheads and headed home.

Now one thing I disliked about fishing was the cleaning. However like it or not, once you caught them you clean them, especially during the Depression. We put our fish bucket in the backyard. Dad ran a nail through the bullhead's back near the eye level on the clothes post, then with the pliers he pulled the skin down from neck to tail. He had previously opened the gut and cleaned out the innards, leaving a slit to the tail. So now all he did was complete the skinning by cutting off the tail, taking the fish off the nail, and removing the head. Perfect, ready for the skillet. He had already scaled the bass, removing the guts and head, which completed the fish cleaning. I helped him bury the mess in the backyard. We really had a very small backyard, a clothes line area and that was it. Our rental was just about ten feet off the sidewalk and then another ten feet to the street, a very small lot for a large two-story with attic flat.

The attic was a dark empty area with a high sloping roofline. It did have windows, which was great. Sunny came over so we zoomed up to the attic. We had made parachutes out of string and old rags. Then we attached old toy soldiers Sunny had gotten as gifts. He was so lucky to have parents with money.

We opened the window and let fly with the parachute soldiers, which floated down perfectly. We took turns running down the steps to retrieve them and do it all again. Once while I was picking them up our neighbor, a kind older man, noticed Sunny hanging out the window. That was what one could expect from Sunny, always testing the boundaries of life. The old man called up to him, "You may be joining the angels soon, young fella, unless you've got wings hidden under that shirt." Sunny was his usual careless self and pretended to be losing his grip on the edge of the window. The old man just shook his head and mumbled to me, "Young idiot—they never learn until too late." Later that summer the old man died. I always liked that man; he made me feel more secure and worthwhile whenever I saw him, he always said, "Hi" or "Hello, young fellow."

It was during this summer after Mother was better that several things happened. She lost her job and shortly after that we had several guests. Two were young Indian lads about twelve and fourteen and one was a Caucasian man about seventeen. The man had a clubfoot. As I recollect they were all handsome and well-built fellows. Mom and Dad put them up on cots, using part of the flat. It was crowded with one bath but we made it somehow. I can remember that she was given support money for feeding and housing them. This brought a new light into my life, having other males present. During the day the Indian lads were gone, being at the house only at night. The other fellow, named Frank, stayed all the time and stayed on after the summer ended. He was given work under a program to provide job opportunities. He and I became good friends, although the Indian lads were very reserved yet friendly. Frank was built like a tank, with great muscles. He resembled that ad for Charles Atlas. Since I was going on eight, I was developing tall but not too muscular, I guess average for my age. He had a football so he, Sunny, and I would throw that football for hours. I liked Frank.

My two sisters were enthralled with all the male support in the house, and I could tell their demeanor had changed remarkably with the addition of these paying guests that summer. Mother was very fond of boys, so her demeanor also changed remarkably for the first time since our tragic move to uptown. She was kept busy with chores at Grandmother's, our house, and with the newcomers. To my memory that summer managed to cover over the feeling of despair that you could imagine was in the mind of a seven-year-old going on eight next summer. We grew up fast back then. Tension was always in the air—figure hearing about a lack of money, bills of all sorts, and a need for decent clothes; listening to the father come home with unpleasant news about work, being cheated out of pay for a part-time job, waiting to be called if work was available, and the constant struggle to make ends meet on utilities, rent, and food.

Late that summer I was in the kitchen with my sisters. They had made a cake, and it smelled delicious. To this day, at seventy-eight I still love cake— oh so good. My dad had secured work with a thing called the Works Project

Administration (WPA). He was sitting in the kitchen and I saw tears flow down his cheeks. He had a statement of pay, and I heard him tell my mother something like, "Eighteen dollars for all that work." Now to this day I do not know whether that was happiness or sadness he was expressing. It was the first and last time I ever saw my dad cry. It disturbed me greatly since I had that child's feeling of despair—or was it happiness? Dad and Mom went into the bedroom and I was left wondering.

Anyway, it did not solve our problems, since his work was sporadic. The ultimate result would happen the following spring.

There is always something to move bad clouds away for a day or two. Sunny and I had fun. He had a BB gun—WOW! On many occasions Sunny took a meal down to his dad. It was a long walk down the tracks to the train yards where he was a switchman. With the BB gun Sunny and I walked to his switch station along the tracks next to the lake. His station was away from the lake since it curved south and we were walking east. His dad was a nice man and quite large. Sunny gave him his food and asked where the rats were mostly available. His dad pointed to a boxcar down the way east. It was visible about a city block away. Sunny was used to this sport so we hiked down there, took a perch atop a flat car which faced the boxcar, and waited. Sunny was ready and experienced, but I had never shot a BB gun. A big rat was sighted coming out from under the boxcar. Sunny fired and bingo—a wounded rat hauled its butt back under the car. We waited awhile and all of a sudden I heard more. Two then three rats started moving along the side of the boxcar in plain view, moving parallel to the tracks. Sunny shot twice and two rats lay quivering on the gravel. Then he handed me the gun. I had no experience with BB guns, so he showed me how to hold it, take aim, and fire. I did this, but I lacked the experience of sighting, so no dead rat. We spent about two hours shooting and finally I did manage to hit a rat. He had shown me how to sight a still target and how to lead a moving one. In all, it was a great day and fruitful since rats were and still are considered a scourge to humanity. Twenty-five years later I had a part-time job supporting my family working for the makers of the world-famous rat killer Warfarin.

We started back home walking along the tracks. Sunny had some pennies in his pocket, which he always pilfered from his mom. He had a grand idea. "Lets put the pennies on the track for the train to run over." Our good fortune was evident in the arrival on the way home of a long freight train. Sunny put two pennies on the track and we waited. Soon the giant engine arrived, running right over the pennies. The wait was worth it, for here the trains ran slow due to being in town. There were the pennies, flattened but not really flat, sort of curved too. How wonderful they looked. Sunny gave me one and it was just a sight to behold. I had it for a long time but it, as well as many of my treasures, disappeared during my long deployment in WWII, since the home I left was never was the same.

On our way home we enjoyed throwing stones along the track and walking up into a small forested area between the tracks and the street that bordered the tracks. The backs of houses could be seen, however there was at least seventy-five yards of land reaching up to the backyards of those homes. Due to the railroad's right of way, that land was mostly trees and brush, and since the elevation up to those backyards was so high, the homes had a good view of the lake and a limited view of the tracks. A few years later when we had moved two more times, I spent a considerable amount of time in that wooded area, then called Hobo Jungle.

That wonderful fulfilling summer was coming to an end. School lurked on the very near horizon, in about three weeks, and my sisters and I began preparing. Cres had graduated from eighth grade with a perfect report card, heading on to high school, which was just one block away from my grade school. It was not a Catholic school. She had been offered a one-year paid tuition to the Catholic school but we were too poor to accept it. Her grade point average was 4.0. Mary would be in sixth grade and I in second.

Our journey to school would be about three blocks longer than from our previous house, with Cres having one more block to high school. We could all still go together. For Mom it was a chore since we all had grown. Clothes were needed, shoes, you name it. I became aware of the fact that Dad was buying kits to repair the soles of our shoes from those uptown 5- and 10-cent stores. One evening I was with him in the basement and watched as he repaired the girls' shoes with those rubber soles. He trimmed them and then carefully roughened the soles and heels and applied paste. The soles were then carefully placed on the wet paste and pressured on. Dad had one of those metal models for shoes he worked on. One time when I came home with a hole in my sole, Dad had no kit so he cut tin from a can, carefully fit it in the shoe, put some heavy pasteboard over it, and off I went. Eventually he did obtain a kit and repaired the shoe. I made a funny sound on the cement walks with that tin.

At this time my mom had a friend around the corner and down Doty Street whose husband, a barber, cut hair at home on weekends. He charged twenty-five cents. That was where I went to have cuts. He was a WWI veteran who had been gassed in war. I liked him because he was always kind to me. He had a son older than me and naturally he went to the Irish school.

There was something I learned at that time—if you did not go to that Irish school, your chances of being "in" were "out." Well, I had Sunny and for now was satisfied.

We headed off to school. My sister, Mary, would wait for me after school to walk home together. She was equally as bright as my older sister, Cres. What was it that made them so smart in school? I was to find out some time later. Second grade was just across the hall from first and looked exactly like the other room with the exception of more books and more black boards. Dressed in her black habit with the covered head, Sister was somewhat younger than my previous first grade teacher. However she was no sweeter, moderate, or mother-like. She was a nun trained to teach. We went back to morning mass—line up in the hall, march down the sidewalk to the church and past the playground, then into church; no talking and no turning. A snap of a rubber band meant we had marched to the proper set of pews for our grade, stop; a snap of the rubber band, genuflect; a snap of the rubber band enter the pews one at a time, so many to a pew; then enter the next pew and back and back till all were standing in the pews. Do not talk, do not turn; a snap of the rubber band, sit.

Well that was it. Then, of course, the priest with his four servers marched out and mass began. It lasted about forty-five minutes and for those who talked, fidgeted, or did those nasty things seven- and eight-year-olds (especially boys) do, sister had a list written in her head. The mass ended and the priest left the altar. Snap of the rubber band, stand; snap, leave pew, line up; snap, genuflect; snap, turn around; snap, march out of church.

Back in school the sister read off a list of those who had committed infractions of her rules. Their names were on the board and a stern warning was given that the next time would be followed by disciplinary action. What was that? This system went on, however it inflicted fear on we young children of Catholic parents. Gradually the list, except for one or two, disappeared. Fear is a mighty tool for seven and eight year olds.

We were not of Holy Communion age, so we were not subject to Holy Communion at mass in the morning like grades five and above. Those kids had to fast until after mass and then had a snack to hold them over.

Because of my height I was in one of the last seats in the room along with all the other tall boys and girls. This was true enough in all eight grades for me. This proved my undoing eventually. Sister made it known that certain children were special since the records of first grade effort had shown their performance was worthy of notice. Now I thought of it during that time because my parents were well aware of power and glory always provided to children to parents who were prominent in the church. I also wondered, since I had some relatives prominent in the church, if that was a factor in my standing. No. The factor was social status and money. Well, let's be honest—the church required money to survive, and nuns worked for housing, food, and essentials. At that time their parents provided what we consider "proper" living, like travel, entertainment, etc. So the church operated like any other business, catering to those who supported the religious orders and to their needs. My family had no standing. We were very poor; in fact many times destitute. Yes, we had some help from Grandmother, but she was limited at that time, too. So in school I was just a student, no favors and no special attention except that my sisters were brilliant. I could never meet my sisters' standards—I had a problem which was becoming increasingly evident.

My sister in the sixth grade was not happy. Even with her remarkable intelligence she was always distraught. She cried on the way home and she and Mom went into the bedroom. Soon they came out and she was somewhat resolved to accept whatever had happened. Years later I found out what happened. When my wife and I and Mary attended the funeral of my aunt, a nun of over fifty years in the order was being laid to rest, another nun came up to my sister and apologized. This travesty happened in 1936, and my aunt was buried in 1988. Apparently the old nun had criticized my sister on her shabby clothes and told her to come to school dressed up. Oh money, what filthy power you have! Thank God for time and tide because it washes away tears. The ruts and garbage are finally buried, only to emerge if one digs too deep or someone else moves the pile.

Back to my problem—I could not see the board clearly. As I remember at that time, I did not tell my mom or dad. Maybe I thought it was natural. My vision seemed to have decreased so slowly in strength perhaps I was not fully aware of the problem at age seven. So school commenced with after school study of the Latin mass. To a seven-year-old this is monumental—over and over and over again reciting the Latin mass as it pertains to the server. Those priests and nuns were fortunate to have such a willing group of slaves. That was somewhat true because they had the full support of our parents.

However, thanks to our great God, there is always one who provides needed entertainment in situations of child stress. That was a new sort of friend, James. I did not know where he lived but I did know his dad had a good job. Jim made me laugh. He did things that were just right for a real boy—he put girls' pigtails in the ink wells, he stuck out his tongue when Sister turned her back, he made funny faces, and he always was kind to me.

He and I usually served mass together. That time came in the fourth grade, to be discussed later.

Since Cres was now in high school, she no longer walked home with us. Mary and I would be on our own and since the main street off the capitol square was right in front of us when we left school, we would look at the movie marquees and store fronts and amble along enjoying the sights. It was a long way to walk in bad weather and that was right around the corner. We were all growing taller, which meant more clothes. Frankly, I cannot imagine how Mom and Dad were providing. I know there were several agencies for the poor that Mother went to. There were many poor families in our school and in my class; probably 20 percent were considered poor. In second grade we were included in the sing-a-longs provided by a professor from our local university. He was a gray-haired man, sort of chubby. I always thought of him as our Santa Claus.

Dr. Gordon was a dream come true. He was funny, he was talented, he sang, and he laughed. He was a music instructor, a leader in music, a conductor, and he was brilliant.

I looked forward to his weekly stay, which only lasted about thirty to forty minutes to lead us in music and tell us about the beauty of using your voice to make yourself and others happy. It was probably the best time I had in that school over the eight years of my grade school education. He came every year and I loved him. When he was there everyone smiled and laughed. He taught us and led us in kids' songs. I loved to sing. Good or bad, I had no idea but it was fun and that is what we really needed. Now, looking back, I realize how much those visits filled a dark void in my early years with a bright shining light.

During that fall and winter, Dad had sparse work as I recall. Those fishing poles were used weekly until the lake was frozen over. I really enjoyed sitting with him just quietly, smelling his cigar smoke, listening to him hum and sing tunes of the day. We rarely came home without at least one or two fish. I really had a hard time cleaning them. Dad was so good at cutting and scaling them. He was skeptical of my using the small pocket knife since as a boy he had been in a circle of lads playing flip the knife. One of the boys in flipping the knife had it lodge in his eye that he ultimately lost in surgery. That really scared me so I have always been careful of small knives. His skill was gleaned when he was a lad and from a poor family, since his responsibility was bringing home fish. He had an older brother and seven sisters, with him being the youngest. His father, a carpenter, was also a hunter who was gone for long periods of time. Dad was skilled in survival.

When Granddad's father died, my mom told me we would see him at the funeral parlor. We were picked up by one of Dad's relatives in their car. It seemed everyone had cars but us. The funeral parlor was filled with relatives talking about Granddad. I remember there were a few who were not polite to Dad and Mom. Many years later that great mystery of resentment became apparent. Granddad looked beautiful. His white beard and white hair framed a tranquil old man in peace, sleeping with his Maker. I had never had the opportunity to be with him or meet him for a get-together, or Grandmother. That was sad and bothered me since I never met my mom's grandfather either. But that is life—just live with it with wonder and concern. How sad.

In those days, for families that had little to begin with, the shock of having less and less gradually was accepted as a "sign of the times." Today the outcry would be horrendous, but I remember no such outcry other than speeches on the radio of what the government would do. Acceptance became the rule.

There was talk of a school noon lunch program. Well, it came to pass. The mothers would host the meal, and it would be available starting after Christmas. Children would be furnished with a basic noon meal, which sounded nice.

That winter was fairly mild in comparison with the regular winters in Wisconsin. Our Saturdays and Sundays were always looked forward to as a blessing. My sisters had housework to do with Mother supervising their activities closely. I was, more or less, free to be with Sunny and pursue our relentless search for more exciting avenues of freedom. When snow was plentiful we had great fun down at the park throwing snowballs at everything from birds to trains. Our rat killing always was a sport, with Sunny's dad showing us the rats' hideouts in the boxcars. The lake was ice covered but always treacherous. If the ice fishermen were out we would feel safe, yet we did see a car half in the ice one day. The driver had extricated himself just in time. There were springs in the lake and above those springs the ice was not safe. Each year someone would go into the lake either in a vehicle or just ice skating or walking. It paid to be cautious, so we stayed off the ice.

Our second floor was vacant and all the time we lived there it stayed empty. My sisters used to dust mop up there, and maybe that was a deal in our rental agreement since it was vacant for rent. They were up there one evening and called for my mother and father. When they came down I heard talk of, "Why do they run around naked?" Seems the neighbors threw parties where people ran around naked. I remember my mom—not my dad—tell the girls to do the work up there in the daytime from now on, but it sounded interesting to me.

My sisters baby-sat the neighbor's girl at our house. She was about eleven years old and it did provide my sisters with some money. They got along fine. I remember they used some of that money to take the three of us to the movies, which was always a thrill.

We all have incidents that cause one to wonder. I had two such incidents, the first in that house. The young girl my sisters baby-sat for would sometimes play with me. She would chase me around that vacant flat for hours playing tag and games that she would bring over from home. We had lots of fun. I was seven at the time and she was eleven or twelve.

One day I hid in a closet and she found me. She said, "Let's lie down and rest in here." I believe her imagination and inquisitiveness were well developed. This time she undid my shorts and shirt and really examined me completely. Her investigation satisfied, she gave me a big kiss and we went on playing.

When I played with Sunny next time I told him and he said, "That's just like a girl—they are always after boys." Sunny was so fun to talk to and knew everything right on.

During this time my dad and mom took me to a beautiful brick house on the lake south of our house. There were many relatives there and in the front room was a box, which I learned was a casket. My dad's mother had died and this was another introduction to dead people. She looked like an older gray-haired woman asleep. We all said the rosary; we listened to Dad's oldest sister talk, and then went home. There was a mass later which Dad and Mom attended. We rarely met with Dad's family, as I reflect—too bad.

My grandmother used to love movies. Occasionally she would take me to the movies in the afternoon during the summer. This started when I was about six. We would walk to a movie theater that charged a nickel in the afternoon. Usually they would be westerns and once in a while a romance. It was great fun. Grandmother was our lifesaver during the Depression. Years later my sisters and I would see movies together, that was after they left school and had jobs.

We only enjoyed outside activities if someone took us and that was not often. Christmas time came; our money situation was bleak as usual. Sunny and I spent most of our free time down by the tracks playing in the snow or with other children who were interested in snowball contests. Nothing wears you out more than throwing snowballs and running for your life while dressed in those heavy winter clothes. Mom had an ability to find used clothes, but some of them must have made us look funny because there were many comments I heard about our dress. The best part of Christmas was eating at Grandma's. We children were always told to not eat too much, especially the meat. I guess we could all starve to keep my mother's pride in repair. I cannot remember presents at Christmas in those Depression years; it was just known there was no money for practically anything but food and coal.

So Christmas came and then we went back to school. I had received a pair of bright yellow tennis shoes and even I thought they were strange. I guess they were new but I never saw them in a bag, they just were in a pile with other assorted clothes. I did not wear them until spring since the snow was quite deep.

The old routine commenced. We second grade boys were being prepared for serving, so Sister took us over to the church and those areas reserved for servers, sisters, and priests. Strict rules were presented in what and what not of touching—certain things could only be touched by the priest. That instruction was quite impressive to the mind of a seven-year-old going on eight.

We also were taken to the main altar areas. There stood my great-grandfather's immense altar, floor to ceiling with statues of saints and angels. It sure did not provide any solace, financial support, or any other kind of social or psychological support for me or my sisters during those eight years of education. No, it brought nothing and nothing was what we got. Education, yes, but no other benefits.

The routine of serving was always practiced with the thought of "do not embarrass the priest, God, or yourself. Remember, they, the congregation, are watching you. Perfection is the rule." Well, I never saw perfection but we all tried.

My sister, Mary, just loved school. She was so bright and charming and rarely was anything but sweet. It made my life tolerable, since I could tell her of my fears of failing in school or church. I believe the pressure exerted on the boys, especially those from poor families, was repressive. She was just one more year away from high school so in my mind I felt the eventual loss of her being available to me as a support. Cres, now in high school, was only seen at home. She was now in a different climate and Mary and I could see the change, like moving from child to adult in one month.

I tried hard in school but could not see the blackboard properly. In fact, by springtime it was even worse. The school announced they were going to have a school nurse available next year, something to do with medical requirements for students. I was still in the very last seat, but when I approached the board I could see fairly well, so if I had been in a front seat there would have been no problem. That did not happen. It always seemed to me that the kids whose parents were rich—some filthy rich—had front seats. I must not dwell on the dark thoughts conjured up by events as they occurred yet favoritism was evident. My report card was always average and my sisters were always perfect, whether in grade or high school.

Sister had told us how heaven looked. She said, "Heaven is huge and at the top sits God with Jesus on his right and Mary at his left. Below Jesus are all the popes, and then going down are the various kinds of cardinals. Below them are the bishops, and then all the saints and priests, then the nuns, the martyrs, the missionaries, and the various orders of men and women who served the churches. Finally are all the people who were Catholic lay people in order as they served the various churches." Well I saw that pyramid in my mind and with my bad eyesight, wondered if I did get to heaven, would I see anything or would they even know that I was there? Talk about frustrated!

CHAPTER 5:

1932: Henry Street, Eight to Nine—Oh Growing Up

There was something brewing at home, with talk of bills for coal and utilities plus rent not paid. Things were not good. Mom was constantly upset. We still had Frank with us. He and I were like brothers, and with Sunny my plate was full. However, rumors of moving were heard. Whatever the problem, it became apparent that we would be forced to move in the spring or summer. How, I wondered, could we get by in another flat if we could not pay the rent here? A young mind just gave up. Wait and see.

Second grade went by extremely fast. My dad sang in the chorus every Sunday, so he and I went to mass together. Since the choir had a choir loft I was allowed to sit up there while Dad sang. It was like being in heaven. I looked down on the congregation and priest and servers. I loved church music and I could hear Dad's voice all the time. It was great. During all the time I spent in that Catholic school, I went to church with Dad except when I had to serve or attended mass with my class or other servers.

When we walked to church, Dad would smoke his cigar—or should I say he *chewed* his cigar. Whatever, he lit it and then when it went out he continued to chew. Each Sunday as we arrived at church he would put the unused part on a ledge he could reach which held a small statue. One Sunday when we came out of church the end was gone. He reached up and it had been pilfered. Boy, was he mad.

Usually, in good weather, we would then walk down to Greenbush. Greenbush was an Italian community so designated since the city had been settled. We would go to a two-story house with a steep back staircase. Dad would knock on a metal door and a small window would open. Then we would enter. It was during Prohibition and I was unaware of that meaning. Dad would have a beer and shot, and he would have me served a small glass of beer. At home Dad would usually give me a shot glass of beer when he drank each night. So I was used to that formality. It was really fun; the men would talk and joke and play cards. We would stay about an hour or two and then walk home. This occurred about once a month for some period of time. It did not seem unusual to me and frankly I enjoyed it.

In second grade our recess was fifteen minutes in both the morning and the afternoon, strictly watched by one or more nuns. There was always a place or two where they could not see all the children and those places were special. Kids would gang up there and tell the weirdest stories ever. Some about families—theirs or others—some about things they did—true or untrue—and most about other students. I was the butt of most jokes in class. There were several rich kids who constantly harassed me. When I finally wore the yellow tennis shoes to school they hooted and hollered at me, saying, "Look at dummie's shoes—they stink," etc. How could I ignore that? At that time I just hurt all over. They also called me "big nose" and other such unkind things. I always thought, *Where is Christ when you need him?* Rather stupid, but I was only seven going on eight. This harassment didn't stop in second grade but finally it did later.

Of course, my sisters teased me about my nose, too. They would say, "nosey nose," etc., and that hurt. Some of the kids had those little dirty books called "Maggie and Jigs" and "Little Annie Rooney." The pictures were erotic and graphic and always shown in a dark corner of the school, away from the nuns' notice.

Finally school came to a halt—great. It was my birthday, too, and Mary and I walked home in that soft late spring air. We really enjoyed each other's company. Cres seemed to have grown so much older since finishing her freshman year in Central High School. She had a boyfriend who would play a pivotal role in my life, her life, and my family's future life, but now it was my birthday. We did not have birthday parties for others, mainly because Mom and Dad did not have the resources to do it. However, my sisters always made these beautiful cakes that I loved, and there were no package deals in those days. We also did not have presents—it was not expected. So I was a big eight. I did have Sunny come over for cake, which he relished, but he was sad to hear we were moving. The move would take place soon and would be to the other end of our block, just through the backyard, so to speak, from the old Doty Street house. It was another flat, the first floor, with no one on second. Good.

Cres had her boyfriend over. Mother immediately liked him. He had curly hair—her favorite—and in fact from then on it was always "Wayne."

So gradually we learned his mother had died of terrible cancer, although he had a grandmother in town who owned a home—she was a widow—and he had a younger brother, Ben, and a father who was questionable in character and demeanor.

In talking to him, my mother found out that Wayne's dad had a terrible reputation for drunkenness. He was also a very hard man on the two boys, and Wayne reported beatings. Old Otto was what could be considered a difficult character. So Wayne became a part of our family, spending much of his free time with us.

School closed for the summer and we were busy moving. The new abode, another two-story flat, was situated on a rather steep hill. Being on the opposite side of our block, it too had a view from the front porch south to the lake.

Our move, completed by carrying things up the block to the new flat, must have looked like a band of Gypsies moving in. There were some fairly wealthy people on that block and I am sure they were not surprised to see us moving again since we had moved twice already. The piano was a bear, but Frank was as strong as a bull, so he, Wayne, my dad, and sisters pushed that piano on a Radio Flyer wagon, well made in those days, up that hill to the new flat. Incidentally, that piano went for rent in that new flat. Mother was relegated to playing a piano at Grandmother's on occasions.

This was not my favorite time. We were only there one year, one of our poorest times. We were in by the beginning of July. Summer was great; Mary and I spent lots of time at the beach. The beach had been completed by the city and offered a lifeguard during the daylight hours. There were none of the precautions like nowadays on staying in the sun, etc., so we promptly got burned, naturally, then used creams and eventually healed using common sense to not do it again, at least not that season. Sometimes it hits you when you least expect it—open collar, shoulders, legs; we learned fast. We also walked to the other end of our long blocks to the other lake to swim. One day while over there my sister was bit by a huge bug. Boy, she screamed, and it swelled rather fast, so we went home to treat it. That same day while going out to the depth of my neck I stepped in a large hole, which we found out was an old large shaft left there for some reason. I went down twice and then my foot caught the edge of the pipe and I stepped onto the bottom. What a scare! We had so much liberty in those days; there was little threat to children.

I visited and played with Sunny. He still had plenty of change and always shared the goodies the change would buy with me. We continued our fishing off the bridges, but now I was older and more adapted to use of the pole, line, and bait. Now I cleaned my own catch and put them in the icebox for supper. Our adventures along the shoreline continued, only now we ventured farther along the tracks. Since two different train companies serviced our city, they both converged on this lake. The tracks blocked in a portion of the lake, forming a triangle, which produced four overpasses or bridges for the trains to pass over. We walked the entire triangle, examining the dead fish, trash left by other hikers and fishermen, etc. There were always others fishing, especially older men, both black and white people all intent on fishing. We were all doing it to fill the larder. The smell of dead, rotting, disgusting fish was always another rare treat for adventurous boys. It was naturally interesting looking at these things, although I hated the maggots, which got worse in hot weather.

On one of those excursions we happened upon a whiskey bottle which was half full. Sunny picked it up and looked at me like, *Boy, we've found something good.* I wasn't that bright but I was cautious and told him what I thought, which was people did not throw away whiskey, so it might be poisoned or it might be piss. He took a smell and it was piss. He threw it out into the lake. In those days, as now, you had to be careful.

The freedom to do these things was probably the only plus during the entire Depression. Very little supervision made early men of young boys. Our parents were in trouble and we knew it, and we did not want more pain and agony in the home, plus we also allowed them to do their thing without our interruption. That helped me in later life to go on and never look back.

My friend Frank who had lived with us was now gone. His training period under some rehabilitation program had finished and he was moving to Illinois to work.

One other thing—Frank had been seriously injured after we moved. He had returned before moving to play some football down at our park. While running with the ball, he fell on a stake that punctured his side. Luckily he was not too seriously injured but did require hospitalization. Frank was dearly missed by yours truly.

Wayne picked on me and ridiculed me in front of my sister. She would say, "Oh, Wayne, he's only eight. Leave him alone," but I could see he delighted in it, probably due to his lousy upbringing and the fact that his father attacked him. He pretty much left Ben alone. Ben was his father's favorite. My mother was overjoyed to have Wayne around. Who knows—he might have been the son she lost in her mind. He was older than me and was strong enough to help my dad on plumbing jobs if and when Dad got any. To put it frankly, I never really looked to him as a brother, rather as a person who used my family for his gain. We were his escape port and he jumped aboard. Besides, my sister was a very lovely person but easily used. She was just like my dad and never said anything, just cruised. Mom did all the talking—not a good situation. All in all, Wayne did what he had to do to survive, so more power to him.

So all summer Mary, Sunny, and I had our fun. We walked around the capitol, we saw and visited all the uptown stores only a few blocks away, and we had fun in bad times. At home there was always worry on how to pay bills. Dad's part-time plumbing jobs were few and far between.

School time came. At eight I entered third grade, Mary was in seventh, and Cres was a sophomore in high school. Mary, Cres, and I now walked together since Henry Street was as close to Cres's school as ours.

Our third grade nun was no different than any of the others. The first thing was rules and regulations—you will; you must; do not say cannot, that means you will not, etc. Well, that was that. If there was one thing I learned very well, it was do not question the word of a nun. Now we were ready for some extra religious education. Oh, we knew the Ten Commandments by heart, but knowing them and saying them was different. "John, what is the fifth commandment, then the tenth," and so on through the class. It was good training for yours truly, who made the military a career. "Soldier, what is your third general order, sixth, etc." Yes, they did make you use your mind and often. What was the penalty for not being right? Well, in that situation you were labeled "not bright," "dummy," "slow-witted," or the worst, "lazy." Now that was reflected throughout the class. The stigma of being labeled poor and knowing it and everyone else knowing it caused a feeling of despair. Where you came from, who you were, and your parents' standing in church all weighed in on a student. I saw it, I felt it, I lived it, and with poor eyes, which were there, but unknown to me, for in my mind everyone had that problem. Well, somehow I got by with feelings of inadequacy and some guilt, for was I a lesser being? Nuns would say "Can't means won't, so do it or else."

What saved me was that I loved to read. The library was one block from the school, a Dale Carnegie gift to the city. I loved that library. We had breaks to go to the library under Sister's supervision. My mind was always on soldiers, cowboys, and their exploits. I guess it was just in my mental makeup. Sunny and I were always talking about guns and battles, and he told me a lot about the Indian wars he learned from his dad and others. Books filled empty spots in my life and I could dream of heroes and heroic actions. My mother played a tune called "My Hero," which I loved, and for years after her death tears came to my eyes remembering how we suffered and that we were a type of hero living in abject poverty, always striving to achieve, yet held down on all sides by being considered poor in an age that was crushed by the Great Depression.

So now began actual server training after school. My poor sister had to wait and wait. We were marched over to the church, led up the back stairs to the room reserved for servers to gown themselves, instructed on that particular procedure, then introduced to the sacristy itself. There we went through the religious demands of a server to properly service a priest in the act of performing his religious orders with the congregation. Well that was really a demanding topic. No mistakes—the congregation was watching, so we minded our p's and q's. In fact, we were at the masses and we were watching, too—remember that. Pressure? You bet, yet somehow we survived and went on to serve until eighth grade. Of course following the Latin mass properly, following the priest's Latin invocation with the correct answer loud and clear, they and we hoped was the key to success. Plus this was all before God and congregation, oh yes. Pressure, pressure, pressure!

Looking back now, seventy years later, I wonder how I stood up to that pressure. A family torn asunder by debt did not need any more pressure. Yet the little things, the small joys of radio music, walking and talking to and from school, visiting the stores, and an occasional movie helped. You see, we knew nothing really different.

Also, we were preparing for Holy Communion and Confirmation. The class would participate in religious functions; on all holy days we marched around inside the church and were seated at the beginning of mass. We wore our best white shirts and dark pants and girls wore white dresses. Of course if you had money—well, you could easily pick out the rich from the poor. They stood out like sore thumbs. Sore for we poor, or should I say "sour." Was that glory to God? No, it was glamour over humility. I always thought of my sisters and our rather shabby clothes as more in keeping with Christ's teaching than all the glamour displayed in church. The beautiful priests' gowns, the tapestries, images, gold and incense—all false. Years later while serving in the army during WWII, stationed in the forest of South Georgia, we Catholics were taken to the woods on Sunday and met by a priest who had us set up a small table, which he used for mass. That mass made me feel more with God and was more rewarding than all the pomp and circumstance masses I ever served for in my five years of serving masses.

Home life was strange. My sister's boyfriend was there most of the time. He had a cat, which he brought over and we kept for him. It was a big, big cat, very friendly, so we got along just fine. Luckily he ate scraps because that was what he got. We always had plenty of milk. The more I think of our circumstances, I believe my grandmother helped us out more than anyone ever said.

35

Thanksgiving came and that morning in the back hall I found a huge bag and box. There was a huge turkey in the bag and other goodies, plus vegetables. I told my mom and she was surprised but said we had some friends who shared their food with us. Now I believe those friends were the Salvation Army or some other charitable organization. As I recall, I believe we took part of that food to have at Grandmother's house, which was always fun and games.

Henry Street was not a really happy time for Mary and me. Cres spent all her time with her boyfriend and Mary was now relegated to sharing more time with me. We did a lot of uptown walking in the snow. Cold or sun and shine, it was a great escape and fun to see all the things one could have with money. One time when we were in the dime store at the ring and jewelry counter, we saw three girls come in, stand in front of the ring display, grab a bunch, and run out. Mary and I told the clerk, who had her back to the thieves, and she said, "Oh, they do it all the time." It shocked us since stealing was one thing you could not do. I, of course, felt the old guilt over the cigarettes—yuk, never again. But we had joy in just looking and imagining. Mary and I would go to the library together and on one such occasion we journeyed into the area where they had all sorts of magazines and newspapers. What a treat to see all the things one could have with money. Even better were the stories in some of the magazines about adventurers and discoverers. Mary explained much of what I saw since some of it was above my learning level.

It was Christmas time and Dad was practicing for the choir, so I would go with him on occasion. He also sang in the cities philharmonic chorus and I went with him sometimes. They both were practicing for Christmas festivities. Music is so wonderful and the music of those two choruses was magnificent. The song I have always loved the most is the "Hallelujah Chorus."

As usual, rumors abounded in our home. Mary confided in me that another move was in the offing. My mind no longer raced along strange tracks like *Where will I end up? Another school and strange neighborhood? What next?* She also said this time it was not lack of money for rent it was a joint move. Wayne's dad had to move and they found a place on Wilson Street just around the corner from where we lived, a vacant two-flat. Now that move would mean we had lived on all four sides of one block since 1929, and it was now 1932. Oh well, what was an eight-year-old going on nine to do? I would be closer to Sunny again, my friend. I would also be right across from the lake—well, across from an old school, but the lake was right behind it, across the tracks. That meant I could see it from the front porch, sort of. Well, what the heck. I had nothing to say about the move.

Wayne spent more time at the house; he and Cres were inseparable. She was an excellent student, although he was considered very poor, lazy with great intelligence, but he loved to read. Wayne was eighteen and had already flunked a grade. He should have graduated last year. Cres was straight As and so was Mary. God I envied them. About this time the piano disappeared. I guess Mom sold it, maybe for rent. I still do not know, but these conjectures were possible. What else? We had very little furniture and no rugs except some throws. So the loss of the piano produced a home with very little to clean.

The school nurse was testing children's eyes. She gave me a slip to take to my parents, which I did. I heard nothing more of it and continued on seeing less and less of the boards in school. We heard that in fourth grade we would begin to see movies in our auditorium on occasion—great. Well, that would be next year. I struggled through the third grade learning the mathematical tables—gee ten times was sure easy as was one times, and of course I am kidding. The stress put on learning the multiplication tables was enough to make one sick. Dr. Gordon still came for singing and I loved that soul.

CHAPTER 6:

1934: Wilson Street, Ten to Twelve—Oh Gangs, Oh Bums

I graduated to fourth, Mary would be in eighth, and Cres was now a sophomore. It was practically the first day of summer recess when our move
began. Everything on the Radio Flyer wagon, carried by hand, or put on a
dolly. Wayne's brother came to help since he and his dad would occupy the
upper flat and we the lower. What the girls and I could carry we did. This
move melded two families together. In a strange way it brought two teenage
males into our family—Wayne and his brother—and another older male
father, Otto, a dark figure I never liked. He was a drunk; an unclean, over-
bearing, and perverse individual. I knew Wayne's mother had died of cancer.
She was a nurse and a lovely looking woman by her picture. Otto was gruff
and I thought crude, as facts bore out.

So we settled in. I found my buddy Sunny but discovered they were selling out and moving. It seemed his dad was being transferred. We had some
time to fish in early summer, then he was gone. Wayne, who was always reading about war, guns, armies, and navies, decided we should play out those
roles on the floor of their flat. They had little furniture and no rugs. What
he had was a lot of dominoes and marbles, and I had a lot of marbles, too.
My dad had given me those from what he had saved in his childhood. Wayne
had plenty, so I saved mine and still have a big jar of them. We took the
dominoes and made shorelines out of them on their huge vacant dining
room floor. Then we made ships of all sizes out of cardboard, including bat-
tlewagons, cruisers, and destroyers copied out of Wayne's library books. They
were placed on the floor, off the shores made with and displayed by dominoes on each side of the room. With marbles, Ben and I would then knuck-
le the marble and shoot at the ships on Wayne's side or Ben and Wayne
would be on one side and one of my sisters and me on the other. We played

38

that game countless times, also making more and more sophisticated ships as time went on.

Wayne had been in woodwork in high school the previous year and designed the model for making rubber guns. He had pistols, rifles, and even Thompson submachine guns. He was a genius; too bad a caring father never challenged him. So he had the grand idea of forming a club. I had had my birthday, so at nine I felt pretty old. Look, I had lived in six homes and was only nine. I had lived with Indian lads, a handicapped lad, and now two brothers.

Well, in this sixth home many things would happen which would impact me for the rest of my life. To begin with, Wayne formed a club. There was a huge old barn behind the flat. That summer Wayne started the "Spider's Nest" club in the old barn behind the flat. He designed a flag with a red cloth background with a huge black widow spider in the center. The flag was about three by two feet. He hung it from a pole on the second floor of the club. The members of the club had to be initiated into the club formally. Since I was the last one to be accepted, due to my age, I saw what happened to Ben and my sisters before my initiation.

The initiation had to start on moonlit nights only. The person being initiated was blindfolded, sat, and made to repeat a long written sermon on the do's and don'ts of the club, swearing to keep secret all business and all of everything to do with the club on penalty of expulsion, which was signed and sworn to only after completing the rest of the initiation. The whole deal took about an hour. Then, still blindfolded, a pan of cold noodles was presented as gross worms. We had to put a hand in, leave it in, and move around for three minutes, then walk blindfolded on a plank said to be sticking out of the large front window of the club without stepping from side to side. "You may drop and we cannot guarantee we can catch you." Then they put a hangman's knot on your throat and said, "You are now on a scaffold and if you step off you will certainly hang and be dead. Two minutes standing." You would then be placed in a coffin-like box and told to stay there until they said we could come out, but the actual time in the box was two minutes (the lid squeaked going down). The last test was while blindfolded, stand ten feet from members armed with rubber gun rifles and swear your allegiance to the club. Then each member voted yes or no. You need all yes's, and if it was all yes's, you were given your arm, a rubber gun pistol or rifle. Practice on loading and firing the weapons was during meetings, which was every Wednesday night. Only the officer of the club, the commander, operated the rubber gun machine gun. Later we had a next in command, a lieutenant, who was also allowed a rubber gun machine gun.

It was not to difficult to figure out that some moms near our house became interested in just what was going on. However Mom told them it was just our family involved and no harm would come, but that was not quite so as time went on. Neighborhood children found out soon enough. Wayne decided that we should practice with our weapons down at the lake park. We all marched down there with our assigned weapons and plenty of rubber bands. Now the rubber bands were cut from old inner tubes confiscated from car dealers and tire repair shops. We must have presented quite a scene marching along with the Spider's Nest flag. Interest was generated among the neighborhood kids, enough so that resentment stirred the pot.

There were several teenage boys who decided to form their own club, and so it happened that there was a rival club made up of boys called, as I recall, the Fourth Ward Gang. Whatever, they became well organized and sent a challenge for a rubber gun war to be held at the lake park. Things were heating up. Wayne became ecstatic. He prepared battle plans, increased our rubber supply, made a few more guns just in case, and proposed a date for battle. So it happened that we had to meet in battle. Now they had no girls, and we had two, my sisters. We had Wayne, Ben, Cres, Mary, and me. They had five teenage boys and two smaller boys similar to me. As the day for battle approached there was a complaint from a neighborhood mom. It seemed her son had asked and been refused entry because of his age. Perhaps he was six, too young. Our charter called for no one younger than nine. Later someone reported our activities to the police and I believe it was her. A policeman came out and laughed about the affair and in fact was very interested in the ingenuity of the machine gun trigger assembly. It was revolutionary; Wayne eventually put them on sale at the local hardware store. Although he only sold a few, they were copied and made by a company a few years later.

The day of the battle came with excellent weather and no sickness amongst the troops. Wayne issued his final orders: who stands where, how many rubbers each was given, commands were charge, retreat, squad right or left (we were in squads), shoot for the head, etc. To say the least, some of us were not only a bit excited but also worried. (I forgot one thing from the initiation—everyone had to stand and be shot three times by a rubber gun rifle. The area used was the chest. The pain was minimal but the thought of being hit in the face was something else.)

We marched to the field, Spider flag waving, for our first combat action. We were there early in that wide-open space with no trees at all. Wayne lined us up at the far end of the field, which was a good 200 yards long. We waited about twenty minutes and there they were, sauntering onto the field. Wayne and Ben met with them between the two opponents, came back, formed our line, and told us to load our guns. His and Ben's machine guns held ten rubber bands each. Remember, the rubber bands were one inch wide. From the rifles, which were one shot, and the machine gun, ten shots, the rubber bands would travel about fifteen to twenty feet. The first five feet gave a good smarting hurt on skin. As I recall there was a rule to fall down if you were hit in the head or body, but arms and legs did not count. So forward we went on a howl from the enemy side. They came like all hell had broken loose. Wayne said to charge and we did. My sisters were laughing gleefully, but I wasn't as confident. Off we went, Wayne and Ben into the middle firing those machine rubber guns with wild abandon. I saw Cres, who was just ahead of me, fire and miss so she stopped to reload. Wayne and Ben wrecked havoc, especially amongst the younger lads. One was crying, and one fell down since he took a shot in the chest. I shot as a big fellow descended on me and hit him in the leg, he fired and I felt pain in the cheek—damn, that really hurt! Mary was hit in the stomach and fell down. Their middle force had been decimated, including their leader, who had taken two rubber bands in the face and was down. I was sitting on the ground with a hurting face, Wayne and Ben were unscathed, Mary was okay but down. One of their gang, a young kid was sitting on the sideline crying. The fighting had stopped; their leader was talking to Wayne and examining the machine guns and our rifles. No one had ever seen the way they worked except our gang. The trigger mechanism on the pistols, rifles, and machine guns had their actual operating parts hidden by enclosed wood sides. Their discussion finished the day. There were several sore faces, mine included, but we never heard more about it. We reassembled and marched home. Everyone reported on their role in the battle and that closed the day, except for cleaning the weapons.

We had regular meetings all summer. We also had one more challenge which was put off because of weather. Several applications were under consideration but when school started, the club was closed down until next summer.

Since the beach at the end of Broom Street was now open we swam practically every day. What fun, although I became burnt before brown and actually became ill from the burn. I was so sick it took almost a week of indoors with some sort of cream on the blisters until I recovered. That was a good time to read and rest. However, I could hear the rest of the gang outside having fun. My sisters, of course, had to do the housework. Mom did the wash and ironing, cooked the meals, and generally supervised. Once I was healed I went back to swimming but with an undershirt on my upper torso. The boy next door, Bill, was not allowed to join our club. His mom objected to our gang, but he did play with me and go swimming, we had lots of fun.

Dad, Wayne, and I would go fishing in the evening along the rocks at the lake. We invariably caught fish, mostly bluegills, bullheads, carp, and perch. Many of our meals were fish and potatoes plus greens of a sort. On Sundays it was church time and usually we would have meatloaf, potatoes, and a vegetable. Money was scarce, so I do not know how we got by. Dad's part-time work brought in little so we relied, I believe, on prayer. We all attended church, and Wayne came with us. Ben and his dad had no religion.

My grandmother had a cousin living with her. The dad of that fine lady had left town and Gina wished to stay so Grandmother took her in. She always liked me and I her. When she came around I would always get a dime or nickel and at Christmas a fifty-cent piece. She had a state job, as did Grandmother's daughters, my aunts, and thank the Lord for them because I am sure they helped us out.

Gina had a boyfriend who was nice and kind and also a drinker. He also worked for the state. When they would come to visit Mom and Dad, we kids would get a kick out of her beau. For some reason he was called "Rubber Legs Dewey." Well, he drank too much on weekends. When they would come we could hear the car out in front and it would cause us kids to laugh to see him trying to walk straight on those wiggly legs, especially when they climbed the front steps, steep and many of them. We were all at the front bay window waving and laughing. They would enter and be as jolly as could be. They and the folks would sit in the kitchen, play cards, and talk until late at night and Gina would always give us kids some change.

About the middle of 1933, I developed chicken pox and it was awful. I could not swim, had to stay quiet, and I threw up, too. It was a disastrous two weeks of being down. At that time Gina and Dewey came over on a weekend. I was lying on the front room couch just dozing. I heard Dewey say, "I am sure that a little gin in soda would make him feel better." Gina came in and said, "Here, John, this will make you feel better." Boy, I took that and twenty minutes later I was heaving my guts out—phew! However, from that night on I started to recover so perhaps old Rubber Legs had it right all along. I never drank gin again though—yuk.

There came a time for Dad to appear in a local opera put on by his philharmonic chorus in costume. It was a gypsy opera, but I forget the name. We practiced a long time that summer. Dad had a leading part and I was seated at a campfire as a gypsy boy in one long scene with no words to say, just looking happy. The opera would be presented in the fall, so it was a ways off and we practiced many times.

School started with me in fourth grade at nine years of age, Mary was in eighth grade, and Cres was a junior. Wayne was also now taking his senior year part-time to make up some subjects. So off we went to school in September. I would be required to serve mass under an older server's direction. Also in fourth grade there was more direction in math, geometry, and science. Of course religion was a major subject, at least one hour a day plus the mass in the morning. We would be provided a light lunch at noon, bring your own sandwich and they furnished soup and milk. I had an aversion for some foods; in fact for some unknown reason I did not like vegetables. Now I relish all of them and all soups, but I believe being so poor with sandwiches with peanut butter, eggs, and some cold meat as our fare, I just didn't have the stomach for those good foods. Anyway, one noon when my mother was working at the soup kitchen in the basement of our church, I sat and would not eat the soup. She came over because one of the other mothers had ratted on me and with great pomp and circumstance demanded I eat that soup. I sat there until the other kids left, then I finally ate a little of it and left—how embarrassing. It did not help me with the other kids in my class. Everyone knew we were poor. It was terrible.

I had two very bad years in that school, one was fourth grade and the other was sixth grade. In fourth grade with the Depression leaving so many poor families, it seemed that the schools made lists of poor children from rosters. I was on that list. One day in the winter season Sister had a stack of bread and canned goods on her desk. She called off names and several students went and received canned goods. Then she called off my name, so I went up and she gave me a loaf of bread. We had to walk back to our desks down the opposite side from where I was ensconced, which meant I walked around the whole room to my seat at the back on the right. As I reached my desk, in a loud voice she said, "There is what the poor do with their food, you give them bread and they spread it on the floor." I evidently had a loaf with an open end and a few slices had fallen on the floor. I walked around the whole room, picked them up, and went back to my desk. From that day on the boys in that class labeled me as different.

Boys are boys. With my bad eyes, which Mom now knew about and did not have money to send me to an oculist, I suffered with trying to play baseball. I was usually excluded from playing baseball in fourth and fifth grade because I never hit the ball. You sort of get used to being ignored. Those yellow tennis shoes from last year fit me better and they did not have tin in the insole. Dad had repaired that pair with rubber replacements but they were now loose. I did get noticed because of those shoes by certain of those on the higher social ladder status who took great delight in harassing me. "Look at old yellow shoes, he's all yellow." Great—I really needed that. Even though the sisters were on the school grounds at our recesses, they never interfered to protect the poor to preserve dignity at some level. They always were there if something happened to the cherished few. Well they say, and I believe, to be thrown into the hottest fire provides the strongest steel.

At home the situation was grim when it came to money, as usual. All the kids were in school, and we had two other brothers living upstairs with a father who came and went like a ghost, usually drunk or smelling like booze. Wayne and Ben usually ate with us. Otto had agreed to go fifty-fifty on utilities since there was one furnace, as usual, for a two-flat, and now that we had the whole building the heat was not turned off to the second floor. The heat cost was high and had to be paid. I heard Dad and Mom worrying over it on many occasions. Otto had lost his job as a janitor at the bank and had no prospects for work.

My aunts, I am sure, provided a miracle payment to get us over November, which was very severe with below-freezing weather. That was a Godsend and I remember on one of Rubber Legs Dewey and Gina's Friday night visits, there was thank you repeated many times. Mom worried often about money but who wouldn't after our history of moving.

The season that always, in those hard years, made me not only sad but also insecure was winter. All its extra bills and extra stress from cold led to sad memories.

Dad was not the kind of man who talked loud; he was a singer for the church and the local philharmonic chorus. So on that particularly cold winter day I, a small lad of nine years, was barely able to hear him whisper, "Jack." He called me Jack even though my Christian name was John. Mother would frown at the name Jack since she knew Dad was very fond of Jack Daniels whiskey and naturally was prone to those adulterous references. Even the thought of booze led in her mind to licentious, drunken conduct. So when Dad said, "Jack, let's take a walk down by the tracks," it surprised me since the only time we did that was to go fishing, the love of my life at the big beautiful lake that was next to the tracks. Incidentally, since Dad did plumbing for the Italian community during Prohibition when he was laid off, I am sure he received liquor and money for his work on many occasions.

The temperature in Wisconsin on that day was hovering around seven above zero, typical and natural but miserable. Now how would a nine-year-old know about that in those years of the 1930s? Everyone in the Great Depression was naturally depressed unless they lived on the other side of the tracks, wherever that was, which one of my age could only believe was a fairy-land. Cold weather required coal for the furnace and coal was expensive.

I remember Dad and Mom talking about the cost of coal. They owed money for the past load of coal and now we were out of coal. Dad had said, "We can make it day by day, but it will not be enough to keep it warm like it has been." That type of conversation was not new to me. I heard it all the time in those days, since money was not only dear, it was almost extinct. Our furnace needed lots of coal and that cost money.

Our furnace was a big ugly looking monster in the basement of that flat, a dark dreary place of immense proportions with the monster in the middle. I thought of it as a giant octopus with its tentacles reaching out in all directions, ready to grab and devour anything that ventured down those back steps.

That monster heated both floors through those pipes. There were turnoffs on each pipe but they leaked heat and the second floor received heat no matter what. With the top flat rented the price of coal should be shared, but at that time no such luck. The monster took lots of coal, something like eight tons for a typical Wisconsin winter. The coal was stored in a separate area, a room within that basement. When the coal truck arrived, homes with a driveway to the bin's window were lucky. The coal truck drove in the drive-way and dumped the coal down a coal chute. If there was no driveway, it required the coal men to wheelbarrow the load to the bin. During that time I could hear their colorful language floating through the bin window because it was always fun to see the coal come falling down with the noise, clouds of coal dust, and the smell that only came with coal—earthy, wet, with an alka-line taste added by dank regions of that basement.

So I put on my winter coat, scarf, and mittens and one of those hats with flaps on it for the ears. Dad was outside holding a basket large enough to hold a good peck of potatoes. The day was just about gone; I remember it as twi-light time. The tracks were one city block away, no big walk, but in the cold, about which I heard Mom say, "It's nine degrees out, so get back in a hurry," I knew we would not tarry.

We trudged along the tracks. Dad was whistling some little ditty as usual. He had instructed me to pick up any coal I saw, however Dad saw most of it since he was a tall man and had more experience than I. It took some time to get a fair amount of coal that had fallen from the locomotive coal tenders that ran on those tracks. Dad told me we had done a good job. From that time on if we needed coal, Dad had me at his side.

During this period of time my two older sisters were well aware of the des-perate money situation. Mom tried to protect us three children as moms do.

Years later I asked my older sister if she was aware that Dad and I walked the tracks for coal. She was shocked and had no idea that occurred. The fact is, I am glad. The girls suffered enough with old worn-out clothes and shoes. Meals were put together from leftovers and with looking for money from any source, it was a very sick situation. Dad and Mom defended us from the utter chaos the world was in.

My sisters were extremely intelligent; their report cards were always mostly As and some Bs. I was amazed at how they seemed to do so well, but now I realize they were studious and used reading and studying to drown themselves in education as a buffer against despair and ridicule.

A strange event provided an opportunity for yours truly to make some money. One of the older kids, he was about fifteen, saw me at the local grocery store and asked me if I would like to help him sell magazines after school. The magazines were the *Saturday Evening Post* and one other of which I cannot recall the name. I would make a nickel on each one sold and sell them for twenty cents each. I took the deal and ran with it. My folks said okay. It was cold out and miserable but money was a warming word. I went door to door the first night and after one hour I had made ten cents on two magazines sold. The next night I made fifteen cents. Night after night, right after supper, I went around the neighborhood and finally made fifty cents. This small job I performed for about five to sixth months and I had accumulated a total of three dollars and thirty cents. Some of that was tips. But I had to give it up. Mom said I was out too late and my schoolwork was not up to snuff. It gave me money and courage, because it takes courage to go door to door. I found out how kind some people are and how nasty others treat even young persons. It really helped me when several years later I was a paperboy. The grim winter was brightened at times when we played cards. Dad and Mom got into playing 500 with Cres and Wayne at night. Wayne and Cres had heard of some friends from school whose family was getting rid of an old round table that sat eight with a pull out and extra slat. Since it accommodated others with ease Ben and I were taught the game. It was rather simple, sort of like advanced forms of other games. We spent many nights playing that and other sorts of card games. Most of the time I just watched and brought water to the table.

Since Mom's relatives were from Germany, she was second generation, and there was a lot of talk about Hitler and his effect on Germany and those who had left the country. My grandfather's folks were passing away; also there was an inheritance available to Mom. However you had to return to Germany and take up residence, and no one was willing to go back. The situation there was too bleak. That was the only time I ever heard of some extra money being available to any of our family.

Christmas was the first and last one I recall where we received nothing. We didn't have a tree. The girls strung our two cords of lights in the window with some leftover wreaths. The bright part of Christmas day was going to Grandmother's, where food and fun were in abundance; eating, singing, talking, and games, and I called that a winter break. On New Years Eve, Wayne used his father's old .22 rifle, took the shells out of the bullets, stuffed wads of paper in them, and shot them off the back porch. I saw neighbors come out on their porches but we were all back in by then.

Actually each of us kids received fifty cents each from aunts Gina and Marie. We went up town to the dime store, Woolworth's, and bought some silly stuff just to make it even-steven with everyone else who received presents.

Spring came and along about February we had an early thaw—you know not warm, but not cold. When I arrived home there were three men sitting on the back porch eating peanut butter sandwiches and drinking coffee. I went in the house and Mom said, "Take this pitcher of water out to those guys." I asked her who were they and she said, "Bums." When I took the water to them they talked to me and asked how long we had lived here, so I told them about our many moves. They laughed and said, "You guys are almost as bad off as we; at least we get to see the country." Since I always was interested in what Sunny had told me about the "Hobo Jungle," I asked them about it. They were more than happy to tell all about the place by the lake. I found out it was used most of the time in warmer weather for sleeping, eating, and communing with each other. I was free to visit any time. They also told me they had heard of my mother feeding bums and that our house was so marked. Well, this was news to me and I wondered where Mother secured the extra food. Those guys were really interesting. They talked of how they rode the rails and how they knew where the best stops were. Those were where there was food and shelter, cops were gentle, and most of those places had gathering grounds for bums.

I was inquisitive as to where that food came from so my sister supplied the answer. Mary said that Mom had Dad go to a relief center that was available in town and he told them about the bums, so they supplied bread, jam, peanut butter, and coffee. What a deal. We had bums come to our house for at least two years before it let up.

We practiced and practiced our Latin prayers, our altar procedures, and our duties during mass. So I was assigned to a senior server and served my first mass with not too many glitches since they did all the real work. Our parish had two priests. Our pastor, a wonderful, gentle, older man, so kind, and then an assistant priest.

There were all the special Catholic Church celebrations as the year wore on besides mass every day for the parish population. Also, the sisters had daily mass separate in their own chapel in their residence. One had to be just about perfect to serve mass in that small chapel under the strict eyes of the nuns. Oh how I dreaded the day that would descend on me, and it did. There was an emergency and a phone call brought me to the rescue; "Would you please replace so-and-so tomorrow at the 6 A.M. mass for the sisters." Of course my mother replied he would be glad to, but in a pig's ear—I was not.

The next morning, I was up at 4:30 since I had to walk in the dark and snow the twelve blocks to the sister's house. First I robed at the church, then walked over and prepared the altar for the arrival of the priest. I managed to do my best; the Latin was difficult since that mass had only one server. Father was kind and helped me along and I did it. I gave myself a C+ for the performance. That was the last time I had to serve for the sisters until the next grade. Possibly they were not satisfied, I was not a favorite, or whatever, but it did not hurt my feelings.

My favorite partner in serving was Jimmy the laugher. Jimmy was a character and I loved him. I served with him during Lent, a time we served a lot. On Fridays we had the holy hour; on Wednesdays we had special services to the Blessed Mother; on Sunday we had mass and holy hour in the evening, all with servers. When Jimmy and I served together it was a riot. We did the job but he would make funny faces and say things that in those days I considered hilarious and naughty. I would have to hold my sides with my arms to prevent keeling over with laughter. God was good to me. Only once did I have to leave and go to the sacristy, bent over and holding the vestment over my mouth from laughing so hard. I told the priest after the service I became weak. He said, "That happens from lack of sugar. Eat something if you get that feeling; have a cookie with you and take water and the cookie." Little did he know I had Jimmivitous.

This was the year we were invited to play football after school at the field near my home. It would be a school team playing other Catholic schools. We had a coach named Henry who seemed to be a nice man. Three times a week we would practice. The games came a month later. We did pretty well; won one and lost one. I really was enthusiastic about the whole deal. My mother did not like it, although I told her it was touch football. Jimmy was on the team and we were both linemen. It was great fun, however Jimmy told me the coach had given him a ride home since he lived a long way from the field. He said, "That guy Henry showed me his penis on the way home."

"Wow," I said. "Why did he do that?"

Jimmy said, "Well, I told Dad and he called the rectory." That was the end of our football—no coach. Jimmy returned from WWII and became a cop, a good guy.

The year wore on. Fourth grade proved to me that I would have to fight to keep up with the rest of the class. Now I knew I had bad eyes and that meant listening with intent if I could not see the board. What good is that if you don't concentrate? My English was good; my spelling okay, but my math was slow. I needed help there for much of the math was done on the board and I could not see. Sisters paid no attention to that, they wanted everything by height—tall to the back, short to the front. The crazy thing about all this was that 90 percent of the short kids were smart anyway or seemed to be, and besides most of them came from rich families. How could I win?

They started a program of movies once a week in the auditorium. Great, but I could not see the screen. It was up on the stage and we sat on chairs well back from the screen. At least I could hear the discussion, but I could not make out the characters. Of course when we marched in, all the shorties went to the front and we tallies to the back. The movies, 90 percent religious and 10 percent history, sounded good and it was a respite from the ordinary.

The playground was something else. One day one of our young lads hurt his leg. I heard him cry and Sister put him on this cement ledge to rest. A bunch of us kids went over and talked to him. He said, "I broke my leg." It did not seem to be broken and looked all right. But his dad took him home and that was all we heard for awhile. He did not come back to school. About one month later we heard he had died and we attended the funeral at our church. It was very sad. He had not been in school long and I never learned what really caused his death. His sister was a friend of Mary's and one time we had to go to her house just off the Capitol Square. We arrived and were shown her bedroom. It was immense for those times. She had a canopy bed, beautiful with white see-through material draped over the top and sides; she looked like a princess sitting in that huge canopied bed.

Mary and I talked about it on the way home and decided that some people lived like royalty and we like paupers. The whole world was, to our view, upside down.

My dad had obtained a couple cases of empty beer bottles from a friend who was leaving the city, plus the caps and a bottle capper. He had made beer before in his younger days and now was making it again. I saw the brew aging down in the cellar and liked the smell and the brewing beer. He eventually bottled and capped it and put it in the cases. Otto was becoming more and more abusive and ugly. When he was kind and benevolent he was a different man but obviously something in his life was going wrong besides losing his job at the bank. In early spring he came home drunk, started down the cellar steps, and then eventually stumbled up the steps, leaving his clothes as a mess on the steps to the upstairs flat. We smelled a foul odor, which was just awful. Dad had just come home and there in the basement Otto had defecated on the cellar floor and on some of Dad's equipment. It was a mess. Mom and Dad went down and cleaned up the mess. I could hear Dad, mad as a hatter, using words I never heard before. My mother was trying to cool him down but he would not hear of it. I heard, "This is not good for our children, who does he think he is?" I am sure because of Wayne and Cres, Mom was apologetic. I resented this, young as I was, this was disgusting. We never had a person like this in our family. Mother picked up all the defecated clothing and started washing it. She said nothing, but our relationship with Otto ended that night. He did not work, he boozed, and he was always in trouble with the police. That New Year would see changes. Dad and I also did more coal hunting but spring was there and we got by.

Bill, the boy next door, surprised me by asking if I would like to go to the farm with him next summer. My mom and dad said sure. It was his granddad's farm, about fifteen miles out of town, and it sounded great. Everyone was getting older and would be in new grades; I would be in fifth, Mary in ninth, and Cres a senior. Wayne was completing his make-up classes and would graduate in January. Time was moving on and my summer would be exciting.

Summer arrived. Sister let us know that next year we would receive our first communion and the following year be confirmed. Well, it was an eternity away, for now all I could think of was summer of fun and games. I managed to pass on to the fifth grade with average grades. I loved to write, which was my forte, my leg up on otherwise inferior abilities so I felt secure.

Wayne was finally graduating. He was bit late but he did well and had a fine mind. His manual arts teachers were helping him find work, which was excellent for him. He was very proficient in most subjects but admitted he did not like school.

The lake looked so inviting, however it was still a bit cool for swimming so I spent time fishing. Ben was not a fisherman type; he had friends on the other side of town he was with. This would be the last year of the Spider's Nest. Wayne was too busy looking for a job to be wound up with the Spider's Nest, so the barn was used for fun and games. When fishing weather was bad we kids would use the building for games, hide and seek, cowboys and Indians, playing cards, and just hanging out.

As usual, the day I left the fourth grade I turned ten and actually felt older. The next door boy, Bill, told me we would leave for the farm right after the fourth of July. I said fine since my parents had given me a go ahead. He said we would stay out there for two weeks. Good, something to look forward to for yours truly.

During the first week of vacation I told Mary about the Hobo Jungle. She said, "I want to see it," so off we went. We walked to the tracks; it was a great summer day. We went down the tracks about four city blocks and then off the tracks to the large tree and brush area between the tracks and the backs of the houses perched up on the ledge. We found the clearing that had a campfire and several places where boards were placed to lay on. Also there were lines spread between the trees.

Just as we were leaving a man of about twenty-five years of age came into the clearing. I told him I wanted my sister to see the living conditions for some people during the Depression and we knew of this place from people my mother fed for the past two years. He was interested in knowing that someone really cared. He was from the eastern part of the country and had been traveling west for a few weeks, looking for work. He was really heading for the great west, the coast, where he heard there would be work in the future. We asked him about traveling the tracks and he said, "Don't do it unless you are desperate." There were many railway workers who were designated to get the bums off the trains. This had been going on a long time and the railroads were starting to crack down. We wished him well and walked home. I told him about our house being marked and he should look it up. Mary and I looked for the mark but never saw anything unusual.

Great—the beach was being finished. Mary and I went down and watched them unloading sand and the pier being remodeled to have a nice L-shaped design. Swimming would be far better and there would be a lifeguard. By the end of June it was ready and with the warm weather, the season for swimming began. I got one good swim and then it was time to become a farmer, or so I thought.

Bill's granddad picked us up on the day after July fourth. Since we did not have a car I rarely if ever had a ride in a car. (Oh, I forgot—I did have a car ride years earlier with a friend of my aunt.) Anyway, away we went. I took a few changes of clothes and my toothbrush. It seemed like a long ride, in all about eighteen miles from my home, then up a dirt road to the farm, it was great. There was a big, big barn, several outbuildings, a pigsty and feed area, chicken pens, and fields in all directions.

I met the grandmother and the hired man, all nice people. I liked his grandfather, a real outgoing person. I was quite shy but he loosened me up.

1924: Author and Gina at Grandmother's side porch

Mary, Author, Cres - 1926, Mound Street

Mother and Dad, Circa 1920

Cres, Mom, Author and Mary – 1938, N. Broom Street

Wayne and Cat, Cres, Author, Frank on visit from Illinois, Mom, Mary – North Broom St., 1938 with Fire Station in background

We kids, No. Broom St., 1938

Author, 13 years old, 1939 N. Broom St.

Mary, Mother, Cres, Author, Dad – Sherman Avenue, 1940

Wayne and Author – Gorham Street, 1942

Pregnant Cres, Author – Gorham St., 1942

Author on leave, 19 years old, 1943

Author, 21 years old, 1945
10th Army Central Pacific Command,
Okinawa waiting to come home.

He said, "Boys, go over and watch them milk the cows." We thought that would be fun.

I had never been with cows before, to say nothing of in a cow barn. Bill was still talking to his gramps so I went into the barn where the men were tending to the milking machine and cows. I walked behind the cows, down the ramp, and what do you think—as I passed one of the cows it started urinating just behind me and it sprayed on the barn cement wall, while the one just beyond me started to crap. Well the hired hand and his friend who was visiting burst into laughter. They made remarks like, "Always nice to entertain visitors to the barn," and "The cows are giving you a howdy doody." I was really embarrassed but just kept going to the back door and left. Bill got a big kick out of it and hurrahed me for days.

The next day Bill saw a girl from the next farm over in the adjoining field. He hollered to her and we went over the fence. In that field were several cows and a young bull. When that bull saw us it came running in our direction. The girl called to Bill, "You better run," so we did, just making the fence and over as the bull pulled to a stop behind us inside the fence. I was getting the idea that this farm business was going to be a bit hairy.

The morning meals were great with oatmeal, eggs, bacon, and homemade bread. Boy, I didn't get any of that at home. Then we had chores—to feed the chickens, hogs, and calves. The hogs amused me for I had never seen hogs eat before. What a mess! Just put the feed in the trough with slop milk leavings and how they struggled, big ones, little ones, all climbing over each other. Gosh I found out what the word PIG really stood for.

We also loaded manure into the back of the wagon for spreading. That stuff is really heavy. Also, we shoveled and raked it out of the barn and washed down the floors. I became familiar with the outhouse and the use of a chamber pot in the middle of the night. All I could think of was spiders on my butt or something even worse. And, by George, there was a Sears Roebuck catalogue out there for wiping.

I remember sleeping like a baby. We went to bed with the sunset and rose with the chickens. It was so quiet at night you would imagine being in space. Every day we did chores and had free time to wander. On Sunday we went to church in a small country parish where everyone knew everyone else and the talk among the men was about affairs on the farms, prices, crops, weather, animals, the use of fertilizers, different new seeds, and general news of the community. It was fun listening to the men. Bill's granddad had status in the group and did a lot of talking. He was a great person, very kind.

The end of our country vacation arrived and his granddad drove us home. I was really despondent when I realized I was back into those problems at home, the principle of which at that time was having enough money to live.

However, soon Mary and I were back to enjoying swimming at the new beach and playing cards and learning to play chess. Wayne loved to play chess, as did Ben. We learned the basics and we all played each other. I always lost, being too young, too rash, and having no patience. It was several years later when playing with boys my age that I finally won with patience and experience.

Summer went by. I was eleven years old and facing the fifth grade. I would be on the second floor in the school, up those long steps from my last four grades. Mary was now a freshman in high school and Cres a senior. Time was moving on. Ben was in high school but I never knew his grade. He was in and out so often I never really knew about his goings and comings. Things were not going well with Wayne's dad. He could not find a job and the money situation was always a problem. I knew that something was brewing but had no answers. We all headed off for school. Dad had some luck in finding plumbing work and with the help of our aunts, was given an application for state employment.

School commenced and I was pretty happy with my nun. She recognized I had a problem seeing writing on the blackboard so she placed me in a row near the front. It did improve my grades but of course I still had poor vision.

The same serving on Sunday and for the nuns went on. The one big difference was we had lost our old kind pastor. He was put out to a country parish to live out his days. Our new pastor was a hollering, hell and brimstone priest, large and rough acting. Everyone was afraid of him. Sometimes he was gentle but most often he was in that attack mode and watch out. I got in his sights, as we will discuss a bit later. This priest gave sermons constantly on hell and damnation, shocking for all the parishioners who had the old gentle priest for all those years. Serving for this new priest was like waiting for a volcano to erupt, he was that frightening.

That fall the opera my dad had practiced for was played out at the local theater. My small part of sitting on the stage and looking like a kid was rehearsed and easy. The opera was played on four nights, which meant being there and ready to go. The costumes were really well done. Dad sang a few solos and I thought he sounded great. All I did was sit with those glaring lights in my face, barely able to see the audience. When I did see them, they looked so intent their faces glowed in the light and I had a feeling we were not actually there, that we were sort of floating. The feeling stopped as the last song was sung, then the curtain came down, went up and down and up and down. Hooting and hollering and clapping, we all walked out and bowed and the curtain came down. This we did for every performance. It was a good experience.

My mom and sisters came to the last performance and were impressed, but I was glad it was over.

Dad's singing experience continued for years with the choir. A short time after our stage experience he allowed me to accompany him on a visit to his philharmonic director's home. We had been picked up by the director's friend and taken to a home on the lake not too far from our home. It was a beautiful home to behold, red brick. They went in the house and I waited in the car. Sometime later Dad came out and I could see he was excited. He said, "Let's walk home from here," although it was about a mile. On the way he told me the director had requested he accompany him to South America and train as a concert tenor vocalist. I could tell he was elated for the honor and concern the director showed in him. I wondered how could this be and sort of put it in those words. Dad told me it would never happen. Mother would never approve, and how would we live with him gone. I know they talked; I heard her amazement that this could happen with our conditions as they existed. It never came to be, yet I still wonder what it would have been for Dad, who had a tenor voice that reached the stars. It was awesome to hear at church. Of course, now he sings for our God in eternity.

School was going pretty good. We were practicing for a Christmas play focusing on the birth of Jesus, the arrival of the three kings, and all the animals needed on stage. Practicing for the big event took a lot of time. The superior of the school was making a big deal of it. One day as we were practicing and we were getting close to Christmas, the sisters were moving chairs and sets around the auditorium and stage. The old large piano needed to be brought forward to be near the stage. She asked for the boys, especially big ones, to push the piano. The largest and strongest boys helped; I was there too.

Everyone started at once to move the piano, however like pushing a horse on all sides, something is going to give. The piano moved a few feet and then with Sister hollering, "Stop pushing it's tipping!" down it came. Crash and crunch, as one boy's foot was under the piano. The sight was gruesome to say the least. The noise of that piano falling in that old building on that wood floor with those high ceilings caused a reverberation heard throughout the building. There was stunned silence and then everyone was trying to free the injured foot. The poor lad was in pain and with the arrival of our principal, was escorted out of our sight by several larger boys carrying him to ease the pain. Righting the piano was no small problem. It took the assistance of several men to put the old girl back up and operating, but it was ready for our Christmas play.

The play went on and we gowned in our Jewish finery made by moms and appeared on stage, I as Joseph with a girl whose name I forget as Mary. The three wise men, the shepherds, and the baby, a cute doll, were all frozen in time for the scene of a lifetime. The wise men presented their gifts with majesty, the shepherds made their acknowledgment of thanks to God for leading them by the divine star, the few animals behaved—sort of—and we stars in the middle—the doll, the mother, and Joseph the surrogate father—were admired.

Christmas was a bummer; our new priest had no patience with servers. He constantly was in a hurry except when he lectured on Sunday. Christmas masses had processions that commenced down the sidewalk from the school over to the church. All the children from the fifth through the eighth grade, in the best they could afford—girls in white, boys in black pants with white shirts—marched into church with the organ and choir venting forth that beautiful religious music, all children singing with candles in hands dripping wax, up and down all the aisles to the front row seats, accompanied by regulated snapping of rubber bands by the nuns. I could hear my dad's voice, which was consoling.

The night of the midnight mass came. Father—his name was of all things, Gabriel; I will always remember that name—was in a particular tizzy. We servers had been on duty continuously during the season of holiness. We served for the nuns for the many extra masses and functions over the holy days. The reward was usually a large bag of candy treats. In the Depression anything sweet was even sweeter. We were so young, so innocent, so willing to serve our God, our true redeemer, our top man made king of all. I still feel that way. There is no other person in all of history so tender, kind, forgiving, generous, and perfect as our Holy Son of God, Jesus. I had to say that because I can forgive all the faults, all the insults, all the cruelty inflicted on my sisters and me because of people in robes. The basic tenet of the Holy Catholic faith is Jesus is all forgiving and we are to follow in His nature and footsteps.

Well, that night of Christmas Eve came, the midnight mass where the choir sung louder, the congregation was immense, the mass was longer, the decorations were in abundance, the incense overwhelmed the olfactory senses, and Father Gabriel was in a dither. It went on, and on long, and with his homily dedicated to those whose need for salvation were sitting right in front of him. My impression was always that Satan sat in the front pew glaring at him. But when it came time for communion, everyone went to communion—great. I, one of four servers, went to put the communion cloth up. In those days everyone was served communion at a church-wide very ornate marble communion rail. We servers put a cloth covering up and over the rail, which hung on our side and flipped over the rail. When everyone had received communion, we flipped it back. I had completed my task at one end and had just turned around when the very reverend Father Gabriel was upon me like a raging bull. He obviously did not see me performing my task and ran me down. His chalice of hosts dropped to the floor and disaster struck—he came totally unglued. I made my way back to my place at the altar. I could hear his exclamations of horror and distress. Help was administered by the other priests since there were always several more at these special masses. In those days if you dropped a host, the floor where they lay was specially treated; the hosts were collected and attended to by the assistant to the pastor. What they did with them since they were the sacred body of Jesus Christ, I was not aware of, but now I am. The mass concluded and we servers were through and went down to the dressing room. They all received their treat and went home. Sister told me Father Gabriel wished to see me so I went up those long black back stairs. He was undressing, his robes flung here and there. He finally looked at me and made many comments on my ruining his mass. He was totally embarrassed. My clumsiness had caused this terrible display of Christ being hurled to the ground and I should not expect any reward downstairs. He said, "Get out," and I went down those dark back steps. Sister was gone, the treat was gone, it was almost 2 A.M. and I was miserable, crying, tired, and I still could not see well. Was there really a God after all? Did he know I was here? What had I done to create this misery on myself? I walked home thinking of God, Jesus, the misery of Christmas, a Christmas not like other kids I knew. Just another day of the Depression and I knew mental anguish even when trying to be good.

Now in the year 2002 at seventy-eight years of age, I see kind and gentle priests. There are no more nuns teaching where we live. Children at our church are treated like precious idols, with reverence. The sermons are of hope, happiness, the pain has been paid by Jesus, we should enjoy life, love, live for our family, and believe that salvation is always earned through God's Grace and your own actions.

But then the world was on the verge of world war, and the tensions were mounting. America had been burned by years of depression and families, poor families, had lost hope. The will to survive was strong, children were growing up, and the government was providing assistance for jobs. Some of the young men went into the Civilian Conservation Corps, others on the Work Project

Administration in areas where needed, and the European war was providing incentives in the steel industries to support impending military needs. Slowly but surely the tide was turning.

That Christmas of 1935 caused me stress and anxiety concerning my future in this struggle for acceptance and total value as a human being. It seemed that I would have to try harder to please everyone.

Of course, the action at home was not providing much support. If it had not been for my grandmother, aunts, and cousin Gina, my life may have been drastically changed for the worse. I had a feeling, at times, I must have been left on the doorstep and that I was probably a Jewish baby abandoned by a lost mother. Sound strange? Well, it was not. I harbored that thought way into my late teen life and expressed it to my sisters, who had a big laugh over it. Later in life I realized that the moves, the bodies moving through the house, either leaving or staying, probably caused that feeling. I cannot ever say my dad and mother treated me other than a son, it was just that they were under stress and despondent, more miserable than I.

There were several very important incidents that spring. Otto was often drunk. One night Dad smelled something acrid. The answer was soon evident—long streams of liquid came pouring down our dining room window from upstairs. Otto was urinating on his big bay window and it was pouring down through the wallboards. It was also on the floor, having dripped off the sill. That was the last straw. There was shouting and hollering up the back hall steps. It was evident that things had to change. We could not afford to keep the utilities paid and rent was not being paid by Otto, so spring would see changes. Otto did make up what he called his favorite recipe and brought it down for our supper; it was potatoes, green peas, and hamburger. I never liked that dish and maybe that is prejudice but it galls me.

Sister had my eyes checked and the nurse again notified my folks that I should have glasses to adequately see the board. It did not happen. Times were tough although they would change soon, but not for my eyes until sophomore year.

Before Ben and his dad left for good there was a strange incident. Ben asked me to walk out to the university with him, stating there was a great place to view the whole lake. It sounded like fun so we went. The walk was a good two miles. When we got to the front of the university we were still a half a mile from the area he mentioned. Behind the large main building, high on a hill, was an area of trees and park-like ground. Just beyond that the land fell away to the beautiful lake. This area had many trees and Ben said, "Let's lay here under the trees and view the lake." All of a sudden Ben rolled over me and began to take my pants down. He said, "Just lay still and we will have a good time," and he took down his pants quickly. It frightened me and I struggled and told him to get off. He was not happy and rolled off me, then just pulled his pants up and started home without me. I got up and followed him for a while but then took side streets home. I did not mention this to my folks or anyone else but Billy. He said, "It was lucky for you he went away. That was a close call. There are guys like that." Shortly after this Ben and his dad went away for good. Ben did tell me they had to leave because the police had ordered them out of town.

CHAPTER 7:

1938: North Broom, Twelve to Fourteen—Oh Live Ins, Oh Cars

Spring was eventful. Cres was out of school and was on a list for jobs with the state. Wayne was on a list and receiving help from the guidance counselor at the high school. Mary and I were still students. I was preparing for the sixth grade and Mary was a new sophomore.

Push came to shove and in the spring of 1936 we decided to move, or should I say Mom and Dad did. Wayne and Cres had found a home next to a vacant lot, kitty-corner from a fire station and across the street from one of the older public schools with a fenced yard. We all went over to see it. The best part was the location—two blocks from my school, and three blocks from the Carnegie Library and the high school.

Otto and Ben moved out, to where we did not know. Ben stayed with his dad. We finally moved in June after school let out. We had time to use the beach for swimming and did our customary fishing at night, Wayne, Dad, and I. The days went fast and the move began.

During the move I and Jimmy, my friend and altar boy, served together at morning mass. We had visiting priests since our pastor was out of the city. These priests were very easy to serve for and they helped us with our Latin. Jimmy was always the prankster so he showed me where the wine was kept. After mass he decided to take a good taste and did just that, then he invited me to partake and I did. The wine was very mild and because it was sanctuary wine, tasted even better. I felt exonerated; the unfair treatment by the pastor was now evened out. I had two more shots and we went home.

There are always negatives with positives and so it was with the house. The owner had the right under the lease to use the very large upstairs front bedroom when he was in town. That meant the room was always locked. Actually, we had another person living in the house although we rarely saw him. The main bathroom was across from his room so when he was in he also used it. Fortunately there was a small bathroom off the steps leading downstairs to the basement, a typical half-bath. So we had Wayne and me sleeping together in a back room, which had been the attic but was insulated and boarded. It had slanted ceilings and closets under the bottom portion of the wall. The girls had the bedroom next to ours. The folks were in the front bedroom behind the owner's near the bathroom. So there were four bedrooms upstairs and downstairs a front windowed porch, front room, dining room, small study room off the dining room, a kitchen, pantry, and the stairway to the basement, which had the bathroom and stairway up to our attic bedroom. It was a large house.

We could do all this, the move, since Cres had been selected to work for the state as a clerk. Wayne had been selected as a messenger for the local gas and electric company. The job was more responsibility than just messenger, and Dad had passed a written examination to work as a plumber for the state. He was waiting for a job to open.

The family got settled in and Mary and I went off to school. The sixth grade was on the second floor and had a nun who was very strict. Again I was in the back of the room—those nuns never got over the routine of large to the back and small to the front. It was in this grade I was challenged by the boys in the class, I should say *some* of them, who were not challenged by poverty. On several occasions I was physically attacked on the playground. The first time was just pushing and shoving by a group of six or seven and I was not hurt. It hurt my feelings because they said ugly things about my dress and looks. The second time the small group who always taunted me hollered loud and rounded up more guys, then they hemmed me against the fence and started hitting me. That time I hit back, kicked, and hit. One boy went down in pain, another was crying, and they stopped.

Years later I met one those boys at his home. The first thing he said to me was, "You cost me a nut." The kick I gave him took one of his testicles. Talk about poetic justice.

Everything went as usual. The school nurse sent the eye slip home, but I sat near the back this time in the center, and my grades were average. I loved to read and found a Civil War series at the library. There were about twenty books in the series and I read them all. I prayed I could be back there and over and over saw myself in the individuals I read about, riding the horses over the parapets, carrying the flag, fantasizing roles as I read. So it was that one day the nun asked the class to participate in answers to religious questions. She was asking questions about the Blessed Mother. Now I cannot remember what I said but I raised my hand to answer about the Blessed Mother and birth of Jesus. She heard me and the look on her face was one of rage. She went to her desk, took out a type of tape that was thick and wide, came back to my desk, placed the tape from ear to ear, grabbed me by the arm, took me up the back stairs near the entrance to the auditorium, and said, "Stay there until I come back." It was about 2 P.M. I stood there in fright; it was very dark.

That event affected me all my life. Anytime I was in a dark place alone I would have a panic attack and have to get out. In WWII it happened several times and when I had recent CAT scans I needed to take sleeping pills for the procedure. No one ever apologized to me. I had done nothing; I to this day cannot remember any words to denigrate the Blessed Mother. Whatever it was I know not; the teacher traumatized me. I stood there in fright. It was very dark and I could barely hear the bell ring for school to get out. No one came. My sister was in high school and would come by and we would walk together. I did hear footsteps leave the building but then nothing. I then became panicky. I estimated thirty minutes later I heard a person come; it was the superior. She said, "What are you doing here?" and I told her. She had removed the tape and could see I was terribly upset. I left school; my sister was still waiting and I told her. She was shocked so we went home and told my mom. Mom said, "Oh, just forget about it. It is done and there's nothing we can do about it." That was the way it was. I always thought, when in WWII, the treatment I received in that school hardened me up for my years of duty in the army.

Our class had received Holy Communion for the first time in fifth grade. Preparation for that was practicing going to and coming from the altar, which we were well versed in. The best part was learning and believing in the fact that our Lord Jesus was actually in the blessed host. To doubt that would make the whole event nothing more than a ceremony. This was the real thing and was treated as such. It meant a clean soul must present itself to our Savior for this union in grace. That is a lot for an eleven-year-old to fully understand. Of course we all had our first confession. The instruction for that phase was to learn the Ten Commandments fully, review our acts, and present ourselves to a priest in the confessional as a penitent. This also was very difficult, understanding sin. What was sin? Had one sinned? Were they actually doing a sin in direct disobedience to God? Had they committed the act willfully and with vile intent against God? Well that was a lot for the age group being absolved.

We all went through that trial and most priests were very kind and gentle with these young penitents. Tender minds are easily damaged. Then on a special Sunday, dressed in black pants, white shirt, and black tie for the boys and white dress for the girls, we all received our First Holy Communion. What followed were a nice meal at home, picture taking, and a trip to Grandmother's home to celebrate.

The new neighborhood appealed to me because I had a new neighbor boy as a friend. His name was Bob; we got along fine. We both liked to play with soldiers; those metal ones had become very popular and we both had some. I had purchased about thirty of them with gift money during the past few years and now Bob and I combined our sets. The weather was still warm that fall and we constructed trenches and gun emplacements behind the two houses. I had kept my rubber gun pistol and obtained another from Wayne's gun trunk. Bob and I spent hours setting up trenches and buildings made of cardboard and from ranges of seven to ten feet, shooting those rubber guns and scoring our hits. Then another neighbor boy our age named Joe became interested and he joined us.

None of us had any money to buy any more soldiers or other war-like toys, so we used clothespins as replicas and they worked just fine. Joe had a rubber gun made in the old-fashioned way with a rectangular board, a trigger at the end held by a rubber band, and then the use of a rubber band held at one end by the trigger and stretched to the other end. These worked quite well but not as fine as Wayne's models.

I got another idea—why not use paper money and shoot at the soldiers like in the shooting galleries. So we took newspapers and cut various sizes of bills. Small size was $1.00; the next size $5.00; and so on up to $50.00 bills. We set those stacks of money out and then put the soldiers on the steps. At about seven feet back we started shooting one shot each. We gave values to the soldiers based on how they were placed. When you hit one, you got what the value was and took that bill. We played that game for weeks. Pretty soon we had to make more money because at first we borrowed from each other; however we decided it created hard feelings, so instead we just cut more money—problem solved. We had many variations of that game, changing guns to see if one was better by swapping them, placing the soldiers at longer range or in trenches, adding cardboard emplacements and buildings. All in all it was great fun.

Neither of these new friends went to my school. They were in the school across the street. When school was out the huge playground behind the school was great for baseball and football except that it was all cinders, no grass. We made do with what we had for there was no playfield near our area, nothing like what we had down at the south end of Broom Street. I missed being near the lake, the bums, the playground, and the bridges to fish off of. That was fun. However, we were close to schools and very close to all the stores. One cannot have everything. Of interest, we never had a car, always had to walk, walk, walk, but that would change in the next few years.

We children—that term was used more often in those days—were always playing if there were no chores. We ran all day, it seemed, chasing one another in games or just for fun. All sorts of tag kept us worn out so sleep was sound and a blessing. We had a radio or two and Wayne and Cres had bought a used radio record player. It even had the system that plays records in succession. They bought the tunes of the day; I loved the music. Our evenings were spent playing outside after supper, then in the summer playing cards or reading. That house with the screened and windowed front porch was perfect for summer reading or just sitting and listening to the lovely music. This was the first time since that first house on Wingra Street I was feeling somewhat secure.

Wayne kept talking about cars; he wanted to get a car. Well, that cost money, which was in very short supply. The fun of it was we could look at lots of cars and not spend a cent. That was what he and I sometimes did. I watched many hot-shot salespersons try to get rid of their bombs that summer. It was a good experience for me. He did not buy a car that summer; that time would come next year.

Autumn and school arrived. I headed off to seventh grade at twelve years of age. I would say Sister was quite friendly and she put me near the front. I was tall, in fact almost the tallest in the room, skinny but tall. There was one other tall student who was also heavy and also named John. We were good friends throughout school. He was a quiet lad and in high school was a great line player in football. John lived just down the block so he, my sister, and I would walk home together, many times strolling the main street and looking in windows.

Our pastor was still there; he was even more hell and brimstone now than before. One of my aunts went to communion one Sunday. She was dressed in her finest; she always looked beautiful in her elegant clothes and well she should. She worked, gave vast money to the church, and was unmarried and very sociable. That Sunday when the pastor came to the rail, he passed her twice before giving her communion, which meant she was left till last at the rail. His pontification during the sermon had been on women's dress—how cruel.

Being out of that sixth grade was a blessing. That nun, for some reason I do not know, did not like me. Was it because of some dire thing she knew about my family, or some other reason? Who knows? It is better to not conjecture. You know all your past and that of your relationships depict

68

the past way back. Some people are more concerned with where you came from than who you are. Prejudice is vile; perhaps I was its victim.

Whatever, Joe and Bob were good friends and we played baseball in that field all summer. Neighborhood girls came to watch us, including Mary, my sister. Cres was working and so was Wayne, so some money was coming into the house. Mom and Dad said we could at least eat and pay the rent, but there were no extras. Those who worked gave to the house and bought their own clothes.

We kids walked to the end of Broom Street to go swimming and Dad and I would walk to the lake in the evening with Wayne to fish. I always enjoyed those warm evenings, just waiting for the cork to bob on one of our lines and see the take, just what we caught. One night Wayne caught one of those near trophy bass, a large mouth at eight pounds. We called them lunkers, and you rarely catch them in close to shore. Another night Dad caught a huge garpike. They are ugly looking but fight like the devil to land. Using those long cane poles, which ran at least eight to ten feet in length, made it even more fun. I wanted to put it on the tracks but Dad put it back in the water. Of course I always had placed dead ones on the tracks before. That summer was unusually hot. The local theaters were left open at night so families could go over and sleep in them. We did that one night when it got unbearably hot. It was fun but uncomfortable to sleep in those seats, since you were not allowed to sleep on the floors. We got by at home since we were used to hot and cold without the use of air conditioning. Very few people owned them.

On the playground I had trouble playing baseball because my eyes bothered me, seeing and catching the ball. Once in a while I did join in the games. This one day in October I joined in a game of baseball. I was in the outfield and everything went just fine. With the sun at my back I was able to concentrate on the ball with less difficulty and actually caught a fly ball. My hitting had been equally as bad but this day, for some reason, when I came up to bat on the first pitch I swung and hit the ball. That ball traveled up and up until it hit the back steeple on the church. Never before and never again did I hit a ball that far in grade school. It really made me feel that if I had good eyes that could be most of the time. Well, it did me a world of good.

Seventh grade was more reading and thinking than the other grades and that made it more interesting. Sister was more tolerant of our needs and I was not disinterested in learning what I could. However I became ill. It was a mysterious feeling, like a loss of power, a slight fever, and weakness. It went on for quite some time until my folks became aware that I was fainting quite often.

The doctor came to the house one afternoon and examined me. He told my mother I had mononucleosis. It had caused an enlarged spleen. I had a high temperature and was taken to the hospital where I stayed for seven days. What they did was to provide me with vitamins and a steady diet of vegetables and milk. I was so happy to feel better and to have the nurses giving me instructions on how to stay healthy. I didn't miss home; this was a real treat.

After my hospital stay I had a special vitamin to take, it was a dark liquid and tasted like Brer Rabbit Molasses. I remember it had a lot of iron in it. It was the first time I ate a lot of vegetables and had no reoccurrence of mononucleosis.

I had joined the Boy Scouts and really enjoyed the meetings and challenge. A hike was planned and I told my mom I needed a piece of meat to take, cook, and eat to pass a particular test on the hike. She sent me to the store with fifteen cents. The butcher cut me a piece of meat and I took it home. I knew nothing of steak, never had any.

The butcher had said this was a piece of steak. That was what my directions had been—great. The hike commenced from the school. We hiked out around the lake to a particular area on the lake that was like a peninsula and beautiful. It was an area restricted for public use for hiking and facilities for having cooking fires. The hike out was about seven miles, just a good long walk. We settled in and selected our designated cooking area. I had the steak, a fork and knife, and two pieces of bread. I carved a small wood branch to place my meat on, pierced it through the side, and with a fellow Scout made a fire. Cooking that piece of meat was quite an experience. The Scout book was helpful in setting up the task, but cooking the piece of steak was something else. It did cook, although it was a bit rare, which in those days was more safe, and it was a bit tough. After that walk anything would have been good. Milk was supplied and some cookies. All in all it was a good experience.

The scouting hike happened in late fall. In February the leader planned a ski trip. We would be bussed out to an area around the lake, an area around ten miles from the school. I had no skis so Wayne obtained a pair of barrel staves and fastened leather on them for my feet and so they were my skis. We assembled on a cold Saturday and were taken to the area. I could see the city across the frozen lake. Well, the kids with skis had little trouble going down the small hill the leader had chosen. My skis were a disaster and I felt foolish and absolutely ashamed. The other kids laughed, some of them rolled in the snow. I tried going down a few more times with the same reaction. What a feeling—dope, dumbbell, just plain stupid. What to do? Well my anger took hold so I picked up the skis, such as they were, and took off down to the lake and straight across on the ice, I started to run. That running didn't last long. I looked back, but no one was coming my way, and they were still skiing. The way home across the frozen lake would be slightly shorter but a long way. My feet eventually felt mighty cold and wet. Upon arriving home, my mom took the shoes off. My feet were blue and numb. She was afraid of frostbite or freezing. A hot water soak was her solution, plus some white powder I believe was boric acid powder. Hours later, after a full warm up with some food and hot milk, I felt better but my feet remained sore for days. It was a crude experience, just another childhood insult.

Summer came, it seemed, faster than usual. I had a good year in seventh grade. My sight was still the same, but I got used to it. Confirmation was completed a few weeks before vacation. We all were dressed up. Mother had managed to buy me a jacket; now it would be called a sport coat. I had selected the name Francis for my confirmation name. All the girls were dressed in white with nice headdresses. The church was crowded with relatives and friends and in the month of May, we lined up as usual down the sidewalk and marched into church for the ceremony. The bishop did the honors during a mass, giving special instructions on the value of what we were accepting by confirming our relationship to God. It was very nice; we came away feeling sacred.

I passed seventh grade with fair grades and on my thirteenth birthday felt I had reached a milestone in my young life. I was still alive, I had been to a hospital, and life was looking up, or so it seemed. Eighth grade loomed in the fall. Mary had passed with flying colors, all A's and passed on to a junior in high school—what a brain—and the summer began. We played baseball until I became, even with bad eyes, darned proficient. Hardball was the game. Joe loved pitching hardball; we had secured some used gloves from other friends of Joe and practiced pitching almost every day.

Several neighborhood boys joined us in our baseball games, game after game of hardball, and we got real good at the game.

Wayne and Cres secured a dog. They called it King and actually said that this was John's dog. I do not remember wanting a dog—we had Wayne's old cat—but the dog was cute. It was part police and something else and of course clean up became mine. That dog put a scar on my chin when playing with him, he lunged and hit me in the chin with his mouth. A tooth went through my chin. In those days we washed it off and put a bandage on it. I still have a scar. King died when I was in the army. He had been crippled by a car before our next move and always had a limp and a bandaged foot covered by leather booting.

Wayne went car hunting; he had saved a bit of money and wanted a car. Just up the street was a used car lot. Wayne saw a 1929 Cadillac, a former funeral director's car, having seven passenger seating with side mounts. He and I sat in it, he in the front, and me in the back. He handed me the cigar lighter, it stretched from the front to the rear right over the pull-up seats. I investigated the rear compartments and in one I found Turkish Cigarettes, almost a full pack. The cigarettes were blue with brown tips for the mouth. Wow! I put one in my pocket and gave the pack to Wayne. Later I smoked one of the buggers—wow, sweet perfume, taste, and smell. Glad I had only one. Well, Wayne finally bought that car for $125. It ran but constantly over-heated on trips so he had a big jug of water and added it to the radiator when needed and he was away from a filling station. All summer on Sundays he would drive those who wanted to go around the countryside, with the dog, Mom and Dad, Mary and I, and Cres and Wayne in the front. We must have looked like Ma and Pa Kettle and theirs.

Mother became addicted to that car and became really distraught when no Sunday rides occurred because Wayne and Cres had other commitments and plans. They were making plans to be married one day. Well, I remember many ruined days with pouting and shouting. How sad, but she did all the cooking, washing, ironing, cleaning, and problem solving and wanted her due. Dad was always quiet, lucky man. Mom deserved what she could obtain. She was the workhorse all of her life. God bless her soul.

The problem became money. Even though Cres and Wayne were work-ing, Dad was not unless he picked up jobs in plumbing. The pay in those days was in the range of fifty cents an hour, either a little up or down. The rent had to be paid, utilities, and of course food. Wayne was making monthly payments on the car, not much but enough to cut the budget. So taking trips cost money. Gas was about nineteen to twenty-five cents a gallon as I recall. At that time pinball machines were legal, so Wayne and I played them at local grocery stores. The cost was five cents a round. He was good at jiggling the machine with his hip and we invariably would win enough money to fill that old Cadillac with gas, and it took a lot. Those Sunday trips in the summer could be anything from 25 miles around the lakes to 100 miles out and then back. I believe we got about twelve to thirteen miles to a gallon, so it did take plenty of wins to make it out and back.

As I look back, no one seemed to worry about breaking down. I used to watch that radiator cap, which was a huge ornate job on that long hood. One could see the steam start rolling up around it. There was a problem with the cooling system. Wayne never did fix it. We just took gallons of water along and he would add bicarbonate of soda also to the radiator as we added water. He had been told it was a cooling agent. But every fifty to seventy-five miles, depending on hills, speed, or wind, we would stop and he would fill that radiator. Of course it would be steaming so we would all pile out and wait. Mostly these stops would be by country schools so we would use the outhouses. The girls hated that—you know, bugs of all types, yuk! Of course if there was an open gas station that was better, the problem was we could not predict the stop because of other factors. But with all the problems, the trips were fun and we kids made it so. Of course the dog went along. What a sight we must have been in that old funeral car, the seven of us and that dog's head hanging out the window.

On one of our trips when Cres and Wayne had enough money to secure the gas supply, we went to Minnesota, Mom's birthplace. I always wondered where my grandfather was and was told he died in Minnesota when my mother was very young. He was an immigrant from Germany. Grandfather had worked hard but something caused his death and I had heard whispers and rumors about suicide. In those days that was a big no-no, especially for members of our church doctrine. So we arrived at our destination. The relatives were very nice and we had a lovely visit. I listened to the group as we drove home. Granddad's "suicide" was the result of a crime. With what I heard and later found out to be fact opened my eyes to the truth.

The past covered a mystery as it does in many families. Time goes on with little regard to how it changes the course of history in many people's lives. These memories covered a mystery that had bothered me for years, the references to a person, deed, and problem, as a problem with some other families. No, it was in our family tree and very close to me. My grandfather had truly committed suicide; yes a foul deed, however in this case with a sinister reason. Granddad had stolen money from the U.S. Postal Service.

Granddad had immigrated to America in May of 1884 from Germany. He went through Ellis Island, New York, Chicago, and on to his uncle's home in Austin, Minnesota. There he worked for his relatives for a while and notified his parents in Germany that all was well. He was well educated and handled the English language almost like a native. He was a good worker and was recognized as such by the local postmaster, who offered him a job clerking in the Austin post office. His title was assistant post master. During this time he met my grandmother and was married. Grandmother became pregnant and my mother was born in April of 1894. Grandfather seemed to be doing very well but the record shows he liked to gamble. Austin was a very small town, a farming community typical of southern Minnesota in those days, with a small population. He must have become friends with some local gamblers. The record shows that he played cards with some abandon. Somehow he lost heavily to the tune of thousands. In a panic to repay the loss, he used post office funds, thinking to replace them in the future. However the future did not arrive quickly enough and he was found out. The facts are he took a revolver, went to the local cemetery, and in typical German fashion took his own life. Who received the ill-gotten money I did not find out nor the real circumstances, i.e., who the gamblers were, was he hoodwinked, and was he cheated? I will never know. All I do know is what the Bible says: "You shall not bow down to them or serve them. I, the Lord your God, am a jealous God, visiting the iniquity of fathers on the children to the third and on the fourth generations of those who hate me" (Exodus 20:5).

Grandmother carried that burden, pregnant with her third child. She had borne my mother, another sister, and now returned to her home in Madison, Wisconsin, to live out her life.

On the way home Dad wanted to drive. He had always driven a Model T and this huge Cadillac was just too much for him. We were going up a long hill off the road and then over the center of the highway. Wayne was really nervous and finally said, "Dad, I think we have had enough." That was fortunate. About twenty miles down the road we hit masses of June bugs, they came and came; the windshield was a mess, and we could not see out. Wayne got out and washed off the mess. That went on for at least twenty miles. By that time the radiator was plugged with them. Fortunately a filling station had a hose and he backsprayed the radiator, then we continued on.

Dad was a little upset he could not drive and talked about the Model T truck with the small box bed on back, which held his tools for the jobs he drove to. That reminded me of the times he would stop by our house when we lived on Wingra Street near the park and he would give me rides. He had no problem with that car. Dad never did own a car.

A summer of Sunday rides and baseball came to an end. School was beginning again. I was thirteen and entering the eighth grade. For the very first time in that school the nun was immediately my friend. She said she knew my aunt, extolling her wonderful virtues as a superior of a high school in Michigan. I had a real feeling of being somebody special and sat in the second seat back from the front. My eighth grade experiences were positive. My eyes, of course, still had the same poor vision but I could read the board. This was my last year of serving. The rugged pastor was still there but somewhat moderated and it was rumored that the bishop was hearing things not too complimentary about the pastor of our church. Of course that did cause talk among the members of the congregation. The servers noticed a more kindly approach from the pastor; in fact at times he complimented us on our support.

All in all my studies, serving, and treatment from fellow students improved in the eighth grade. We lived so close to the school and downtown that my sister, Mary, now a senior in high school, and I really enjoyed ourselves.

On one occasion one of the students brought boxing gloves to school. He was one I could tell really did not like me. He was not vocal and from a very well-to-do family, sort of a mystery student. So on the playground it came about that he had those gloves on and the kids were taunting me to go against him. It worried me since things had been going so well and I had that feeling this was wrong, but I did it. Surrounded by hollering boys urging us on, we started. It was not a long match and I had never had boxing lessons, much less boxing gloves. But he hit me in the face, it stung, and the shouting went on. I became enraged and went after him, hitting and hitting with all caution to the wind. Someone shouted, "That's enough!" and the match was over. I was so mad and had a feeling that this was a set-up that went sour. I never talked to that boy again.

At home we had a special event. One of my aunts had found a beau. His name was Arthur; we called him Art. He was from a small town and a farm family. Art was special, and when my family met him I instantly liked him. He was a very, very funny man. He could keep me laughing twenty-four hours a day. She and he were really made for each other. He had obtained a job in town and needed a place to stay. What better spot would there be than our house? As I recall, Dad and Mom moved downstairs to the study and Art was given their room upstairs. He had a job at a local department store selling shoes. So that fall Art moved in. He was my special friend. Since we were on North Broom and my aunt was on the corner of Doty and South Broom, it was an eight-block walk.

Art liked me so he asked my mom if I could go with him to visit my aunt. He told her he could only stay an hour, so Mom said sure. I took my homework with me and visited with Grandmother while Art and Auntie sat on the couch and talked. It was evident to me that those two would someday be married because they acted like lifetime partners even then in my thirteen-year-old opinion.

On those walks in the fall it was dark by 5:00 P.M. and Art would have to go to the bathroom. He would say to me, "Keep a look out for me while I go behind this tree or in those bushes." I did this many times. Only once did I fail to see a person coming down the street since he had been hidden by a big tree and perhaps he, too, was relieving himself—I do not know—he just continued on. Art had more funny jokes and I would be in tears half the time. He was a scream. Wayne did not like him; it was evident.

Wayne had a friend from high school who came around on occasion; he liked my dog King. King and he would go down in the basement where there was a downstairs toilet. One day Bob and I were out in the backyard playing catch when the ball went under a bay window area of our house that jutted out. Bob called me and said, "Look at this!" I went over and there was Wayne's friend with his pants down and my dog on his back. I almost threw up. Kids talked about stuff like that, the priests had alluded to the terrible sins connected with that act, but I had never seen it before. I told my mom but she said that could not be true and would talk to Wayne about it. However I think she was too embarrassed because of Wayne and Cres's relationship and did not want to ruffle feathers. Nothing was done. I did notice after that King had unusual tendencies to jump on people if he could. It sickened me so I could not deal with him anymore. Perhaps that's why I have so much affection for cats. I never liked dogs from that day on.

Christmas season came and for the first time since Wingra Street I felt like this was what Christmas should be like. We had a large tree, decorations, and lights, and we were getting a few presents. The day was spent going to church and then to Grandmother's where we spent all day. Mother had made a special dish or two and we really celebrated. The only distressing news was from Germany. Since we had so many relatives on both sides of the family over there, Hitler's threats for those still there were very evident in all the many sacrifices being made. Little did they know that the monster Hitler would bring them all down.

We played all kinds of games, word games especially. Then there was always the adult conversation all of us sitting in the front room gabbing about everything. Then my aunt Helene would play the piano and we would all sing religious and popular songs of the day and old favorites; it was great. Desserts were plentiful and candy, too.

Wayne had trouble getting the car started so Art and I walked home along with Mary. We were there long before they got the car started and Wayne made up his mind up to get another car in spring.

School was going fine. Sister gave me help with some subjects I had trouble with, which was much appreciated. We had the usual serving responsibilities all through the year. Easter was a special time and eighth graders were expected to be role models for the school. I believe our nun was perfect for our age. She impressed upon us the responsibility to be leaders and that our actions, seen by younger students and adults, would reflect not only on us but also our parents and school. I took this to heart and used it then and throughout my life.

We were preparing for graduation and Sister planned a party for us. She used the basement kitchen area and had a graduation cake, plenty of sodas, music, and religious articles for us. She even allowed us to dance and for the first time in my life I danced with a girl. It was really fun, especially the cake, ice cream, and sense of accomplishment. So graduation came and went. It was celebrated in church with a mass and blessings for the future and an oration from the pastor, who was in good spirits. We had been invited to attend the local Catholic high school but few could afford it. Both my sisters had earned one-year tuitions and could not attend due to money constraints. The majority of children went on to Central High School.

Wayne had been looking and looking for a car. Just after graduation he took me down to a dealer and showed me a car. It was a 1934 Buick seven passenger with side mounts. It really was beautiful; it was dark green. He eventually had a deal on a trade-in and managed to buy it. The dealer had to repair a few items and then it was his. One thing for sure, it looked like a Chicago gangster's rig. It was beautiful. It was 1938; I had turned fourteen and was ready for high school, two blocks away.

Mary had graduated from high school and was out looking for work. She was so smart and sure to find a job. That she did, with the state, and ended up working with Cres so they went to work together.

Dad had passed the test and been hired as a plumber for the state and was waiting for a call to work. His job would be as plumber in the state capitol and groundskeeper, which entailed many things including planting, watering, etc.

Things were looking up. Art was still with us and had found a new job with a tobacco company that had a local office. He and my aunt were planning a marriage next summer so he would be leaving. All in all it seemed the Depression, for our family, was over. Based on people living in the house, if any of those paying in like Art, Wayne, Cres, and Mary left, how would Mom and Dad live? He made zip for salary. That was solved in the future. As for yours truly, it was summer again and I was fourteen years old and ready to play ball with my neighborhood friends.

That summer there were several personal appearances at our local theaters. My sisters took me to two of them and it was really something. One was Gypsy Rose Lee on stage in person and the other was Cab Calloway on stage in person with his great band. I had never seen anything like it and will always remember the glamour and wonder of seeing actors on stage. Now as I reminisce I wonder why our mother allowed the girls and I to go but she did.

Otherwise, my friends and I spent 75 percent of our time playing baseball and chasing the girls after supper around the playground. That attracted more and more boys, some of whom were wild as one could be. They were more advanced in the sexual pursuits, which we all some day would be. One of them was so wild he would take his penis out and hang it through the wire fencing next to the sidewalk so when the girls walked by they would see it. We laughed and had a great time watching him stand against the fence. As the girls approached, he would holler, "Hi, girls, have you ever seen anything better than this?" Boy the yelling and screaming was something. The bad side was he repeated this "trick" several nights in a row to our enjoyment, raising such a ruckus the mothers found out. One last performance caused me to go home and get walloped with a belt by my mother. I was so mad; I never forgot that she would not believe me and I suppose if she did I would have gotten the same for just watching. She was a heller.

One of the boys had his mind made up to be sexually active, which most of us told him was not right. In those days kids from all schools had been taught by the eighth grade that sex was for marriage. It would only cause disgrace and trouble if you violated the sacraments of marriage. The coming war changed all that for our city because the air force placed a large training base at our local airfield. The city was never the same.

I usually said to my mom, "You know how the guys are." Well, there was an incident that occurred which she was not aware of, and it was just as well. Boys will be boys, so during this time period we had all assembled in one of the guys' houses. Dick invited us all over to his basement, which was not too bad. Nine of us ball players assembled on a rug in the basement, had pop and treats, and gabbed about boy stuff.

Dick lived around the corner from my house and was in my school. We were all from Catholic schools and had a common thread. The conversation ranged from sports to girls to sex. Well, finally one of the guys started talking about masturbation. I believe it was Dick who suggested we all should sit in a circle and do just that—masturbate. So in that circle, nine very young and naïve fellows all exposed themselves and did just that. Of course for that group, sin bred immediate guilt, grief, and shame. The act was completed. The exhilaration faded fast as someone mentioned the confessional response: "Hope we don't go blind." Everyone either laughed or snickered. My personal feeling was that my eyes were so bad I must have been cursed from the git-go. It was true though that the older priests used that holy threat, "Pull that thing between your legs and much may happen. It even may cause your eyes to cross or go blind." It was sort of prophetic, especially for us very young Catholic fellows. We never let that happen again.

Well, Wayne bought the Buick; it was a darb and drove out beautifully. No longer did we have to bring water and bicarbonate of soda along to control the heat. Of course we took off the first Sunday, all of us except the dog. No longer would the dog be with us on trips. There wasn't the room in the Buick there had been in the old Caddy. Now we looked a little more like city folk and less like country bumpkins. That summer, just about every Sunday, we traveled the roads of Wisconsin, a beautiful state with gorgeous farms and good people in small towns, real Americans. Home, God, and country; America's heartland and one of its best breadbaskets, with cheese and milk and country beef, pigs, and chickens—what more do you want. The snow is tough but it does kill the bugs, so they say.

It was 1938 and most people could find jobs. Dad was called to work for the state as a plumber. He was happy; the pay was far less than a journeyman on the road but it was steady, so that was a blessing.

That summer we traveled to see Mom's sister, who was the superior at a town in southern Wisconsin. She was so gracious and kind I knew from the atmosphere at the convent that her sisters enjoyed their life. They had a beautiful home next to the church and school. There was a large grape arbor and great trees on the property. They had supper for us and we enjoyed every minute of the visit. Then a month later we visited my mother's aunt, another sister who was superior of a school in a town on Lake Michigan. The sister's house and church faced the lake and school was behind. It was a tremendous setting, however I could imagine those winter winds, snow, and sleet coming in from the lake. However, again we were treated like royalty. In those days visiting was rare for those finally climbing out of the Depression. I really enjoyed those wonderful dedicated religious people. They were really holy and kind. America was richer for their presence in our lives, and I loved them. Some had treated my sister and I roughly but the majority were very holy.

One of Grandmother's aunts had taught Indians in the regions of the Michigan peninsula north of Wisconsin. They were the pioneer women in the holy orders who weathered the rigors of training for their missions and held tight to their Catholic Christian beliefs.

These summer trips were accomplished on saved change and sacrifices made in other areas and they were rewarding for the family. Sometimes Art went along. Art knew everything, and besides, he made me laugh 50 percent of the time. Wherever we went he knew somebody. I swear someone would come up or call over, "Hi, Art!" It was so cool, as they say now. Wayne and he would argue about everything until Mother would holler, "Get over it, you guys!" I just listened. One particular day we went to a park on the Mississippi River. We had our picnic overlooking the river and the surrounding country for miles. There were clean, cool, clear water springs and hiking trails. We visited caves and trails and historical sites. On one of the trails in a heavily wooded area, a large snake—five to six feet long—crossed slowly. The gals screamed and hastened the snake's departure. They are harmless to humans, so no problem. It was a fun time. An uncle from Mother's father's side of the family had met us there. He was a real fine guy and I wish we could have had more meetings with that side of the family. There were reasons that did not occur, unfortunately including our monetary position. On our way home Wayne was cruising along about 50 mph and a chicken ran right into the front of the car. Feathers covered everything; poor chicken was wedged in the front bumper. When we arrived home Wayne and I cleaned that disgusting mess up, no damage was done to the car. Wayne had me help him clean that car every week.

That was a good summer with baseball, friends, and trips. You could be poor and still do happy things. We still went fishing at night and made some nice catches; only once or twice were we snookered.

As the time for return to school approached, my thoughts were consumed with high school. What would it be like? How would I assimilate into the new life? My sisters were not much help since no one had given them any real heads-up. No, they were such outstanding students it seemed that school for them was like going to another home. I talked to Mary and Cres about it and they told me, "Don't worry. Just do what you are told and all will go well." They did explain about homerooms and changing classes, etc. One thing was for sure—it appeared I would not be with the same kids every class, which sounded interesting.

Well it all happened so fast I could only say what a change from nuns and priests. The entire concept of education changed to different teachers for different studies, new subjects to assimilate, so more to study for at night, and a new addition—study hall. Really, how it all gelled together is just a jumble or memory. It was not too hard, exciting, and frustrating at times; another hurdle in life to comprehend, attack, and conquer.

My eyes were worse so I asked the teacher in each class for a seat near the front, which was given. I found the subjects interesting and some hard; geometry was my problem. The teacher was, as reported by my sisters, the hardest in the school. She was fast in her teaching of the subject and I had a hard time of it. That resulted in my one failure in all my grade and high school studies. I made it up in the summer and ended with a B+ that proved to me teachers make the difference. That summer teacher was just great, kind, and understanding.

The greatest part of high school for me was going to the football games in the fall. I loved those games as a freshman. It was so much fun hollering and screaming, and schoolmates all going the same way for one purpose, to win the game. I was ecstatic walking home, talking about the plays, the win or loss, and reliving the whole event. It was great. Fall was so beautiful.

The second greatest events were the basketball games. I wanted to join the football team, however my mother and dad said no. That was that. Dad had been injured in a sporting accident in his teens on a large toboggan sled. Dad and his friends were racing down a hill and the toboggan hit a large tree and Dad was badly injured. Well, that and Mom's insistence prevailed. That was a deep disappointment.

I felt very comfortable in high school and was never singled out as different, poor, or funny looking, or called names. My sisters said they were just jealous when I complained in grade school. I had more sinister thoughts in my mind about those difficult, humiliating times.

Since the high school was just across from the Carnegie Library I stopped in often to look over the Civil War books. My interests had a wide range but I always had a fascination for armies and war. I do believe the German bloodline fancies war and the tools of conflict. I enjoyed the Roman, Greek, Ancient Jewish, Spanish, and Italian eras of conflict. Then I was totally immersed in all the Indian wars, the Revolutionary War, and of course the Civil War eras. I never was too concerned about WWI and the Spanish affair. In later years I became absorbed in the early wars of the Spanish conquering the Inca population in Central America. What more could you ask for since the history of humanity is bound to repeat in different clothing but with the same body. All in all that satisfied my young longings, cost no money, and also was a topic of conversation between Wayne and I since it was his forte, so to speak.

The Buick developed a large problem with the transmission. Wayne contended the salesperson had mentioned the problem when the car was being shown. There was a slight noise typical of transmission-type problems and the salesman had told Wayne if there was a problem, bring it in and they will fix it. Well, they actually stood behind that statement and Wayne paid for the parts but the labor was free. So we took many trips into the beautiful fall assortment of colors gracing our Wisconsin landscapes. We had a favorite town where they made huge ice cream cones, but I cannot recall the name of the town.

I did not see many of my former grade school classmates in high school. Some were in the east and west high schools of our city and some in the parochial high school. One good friend was also named Bill. We became better friends in high school than all our time through grade school. His family was in the meat business and was pretty well off. I liked Bill; he was a wonderful Christian fellow, truthful, kind, and respectful. My mother loved Bill and she said, "Bill is a wonderful boy and will always be a gentleman." Bill came over to our house often and we played Monopoly and cards, read books, and generally talked about boy things using the great front porch. To this day when I see Bill he always has kind things to say about my family. As long as we lived on North Broom, we would go to games together.

Fall started to fade into a hard winter and I had bad news. We would need to move in the spring. What? After all those moves, I was now near my school and fairly happy with what was going on in my little world, and we had to move. What a blow, and where would we go? Art was okay because he would marry next summer, maybe even in spring. His job was going really well. His printing was like an artist and that was what the tobacco company needed as an accountant.

Our fire station, kitty-corner from the house, had the most wonderful firemen. My sisters and I spent many afternoons and nights sitting out in front with them and talking and joking and just listening. They had park benches in front, which we all used. However that late fall there was a terrible fire in our town. Two of those firemen were in the building when the floor collapsed and were crushed by the huge machinery that fell onto them. We were so distraught and many tears were shed. A pall fell on our house since my folks also were friends with those two. Death is always an awakening in one's life, especially for the young because death is so final.

I found out the real reason for our move—the owner wanted the whole house back. It became known to Wayne that he would sell the property to a developer. A small apartment house would occupy the whole corner. So be it.

It would be the last year I would have a very short walk to school, the library, and downtown. If your eyes are poor you really do not know the difference unless you see correctly. Just to be told you have poor vision means nothing to a person whose eyes were never corrected. I now wonder how many wonderful things I missed. Well, the old saying is if you have never had or saw it, you don't miss it, or something. I seemed to be able to do everything everyone did except get better than average grades. Bill and I had another friend called Johnny whom we both knew from the neighborhood. He was a graduate of the Irish school I was not allowed to attend. On weekends we would pal around and wander up and down the main streets downtown visiting the local ice cream shops where school kids hung out and generally palled around together. Johnny, Bill, and I went to our schools' games together, shouting and hollering like a band of banshees. Our teams during my tenure in high school were champions in many sports.

It was a good time to be alive and with the students of that high school, as time proved to be all too true. My heart breaks for those who sacrificed without a whimper for their country.

Halloween was always a great time with the guys I mentioned. We did all the pranks expected—soaped windows, rang doorbells, chased around the neighborhoods, and generally made a lot of noise, and of course we collected lots of candy. It was typical kid stuff. Halloween also echoed in the University of Wisconsin football season. When we were freshmen our opportunity to participate was very minimal. We looked too young to be involved with student activities. We did see the huge bonfire on a portion of the university grounds. The annual homecoming football game provided the impetus for the fire. What an event that year. It was great and did not get out of control. It was not always that way. We also had the opportunity to see the game the next day, which was Saturday.

The university had a Hole in the Wall event for children so they could sit in the end zone for nothing. We took advantage of that offer. It was used for games where there were few tickets sold and lots of empty seats. It did not happen too often but when it did it was great.

Winter closed in fast and I made some money shoveling walks after school. Pay was about twenty-five to fifty cents for a small sidewalk and a dollar for large sidewalks and driveways, too. Studying and reading the books for class did not leave much time for work.

We always attended church, all the Sunday services and the weekly services usually on Tuesday and Friday evenings. For Sunday mass I continued to go with Dad and sit in the balcony with him, listening to his great tenor voice. Dad's attitude had changed since he was working again, in fact in a job that would be permanent with the state. I was so happy for him.

My sisters and I had ice skates. With the lakes frozen over Cres, Mary, and I walked to the lake to try our skates. Mine were used skates Mom had been given by one of her old friends from the Mound Street neighborhood since her kids had grown out of them. We stopped at Grandmother's house and had hot chocolate on our walk over. The lake was as slick as glass with no snow, just frozen over. I had never really skated and the girls on each side helped me do a fair job. They had some skating experience when we lived on Wilson Street. Wayne was a good skater and had taught them. He was working so he could not go. We went way out on the lake, probably three-quarters of a mile, when we heard a loud crack like a cannon shot, then another and another. We could see the cracks opening, not widely, but there they were. Wow! We started back and were really glad to hit shore. Dad told us at certain times in the winter months the ice did crack like that but with the ice at least fourteen to fifteen inches thick, there was no need to worry. Nice talk, but we still were glad to get home.

The neighborhood kids had massive snowball fights on the playground. That year there was a lot of snow that allowed forts to be built and tons of snowballs to be made. There is nothing like getting an icy snowball in the face—it hurts. The pain of a rubber gun hit and a snowball hit is entirely different. The force of the snowball depends on the throwing party; a rubber gun hit depends on the maker of the gun. Regardless, it is humiliating to be hit in either case. A certain form of rage takes over, revenge is quickly born, and counterattack is the order of the day. Many a good friend had turned coat with a nasty hit. However the fun of trying to be the one hitting overpowers any reason to suspend play. The upside is that those rages are quickly over and forgotten amongst gang members. We did have lots of fun.

With all the moves and changes in friends, those living in my family weathered the Depression. Having been humiliated in grade school on many occasions, feeling left out at home by my father as time went on, with poor vision and poor grades, I was now more depressed about my general state of living. I saw and heard other kids talking about their families and their role as a son with his father and older brothers. In my family I felt like an outsider. In fact the image never has left me. Was I truly born of that dad and mom? Sure I was, but I had that strange feeling of not belonging.

The war was raging in the European nations. Would we get involved? Since I was such a war nut, reading historical novels about our country's involvement in prior wars weighed heavily on my insistence to be a soldier without delay. The time would soon come.

So my psychic depression was there, the real Depression was still around us. Yes, we had worker bees in the family but they were setting goals. That worked out rather differently than anyone knew at that time and would affect my life forever. Mom and Dad could not live on Dad's salary. What would happen when Wayne and Cres married and when Mary decided to marry?

Mary was doing just great in her job and had lots of friends. She would party often on weekends and always seemed exceptionally happy. With money she could buy those nice clothes deprived of for years during her school years. I loved my sister since we were so close. Cres and I were great friends but she was just that much older—seven years—that our paths were often parted. Besides, she had Wayne and he was her one and only.

Since Wayne had entered our family as a permanent, almost adopted son my dad had turned to him for help doing plumbing jobs. That was before his appointment to the state plumbing job. I must say that hurt me for I always was interested in his occupation and just before Wayne entered our family, he had taken me to work with him on Saturdays. I will always remember the Saturday I had started off with him to work and Wayne drove up and said, "Dad, I'll go with you." Dad turned to me and said, "You can go home, Jack." He called me Jack but that hurt; I never went with him again. Our relationship from that day on was never as father and son. The next time I had an intimate relationship with my dad was a letter in WWII sent to Okinawa at my APO address. It briefly said, "Come home soon."

Spring came fast that year, it was on us like a lion. On Saturday night the guys would get together and walk down the main street, which led to the university. In those days no one checked your age for drinking beer. Billy and I were pleased to know that was the case, but the only problem was money. I had enough change from shoveling to drink a few beers. We would sit in the student restaurant and talk, talk, talk and about 11 P.M. walk home. Sometimes there would be some of our female classmates sitting and drinking beer. We would often walk home with them as sort of chaperons. One of the girls showed me her protection weapon, a good-sized knife that amused me. She didn't need us guys to walk her home since she could easily take care of herself. Anyway, it was the manly thing to do.

We were so free in those days; it was just a great time to be alive. We honored our fathers and mothers and we kept the rules so all of our families could, even in rough times, hold our heads up.

CHAPTER 8:

1940: Sherman Avenue, Fourteen to Sixteen—Oh Marriage, Oh Money

When we lived close to the high school I could still go home for lunch. In those days everything was bag lunches. You could eat in the school lunchroom, but many students preferred to carry their lunch and eat on the lawn or up at the grounds of the Capitol Park. Most days I would walk home, only two blocks. The walk took me by the church and school with all those memories of that playground and the harassment that was dealt out. Being poor was a stigma, like a mark on one's forehead. Yet why would other children care unless someone in authority had placed that stigma? Now I considered the fact that others in authority had victimized me, had dealt with the cruel hand of hate for those considered inferior humans because of wealth. It was not religion's fault; it was those in control. Suffering under those personalities formed my future life. I would never let authority rule my attitude for fellow beings.

My schoolwork was average and at the age of fifteen I was on my way to being a sophomore. Summer came smoothly into our lives with the marriage of Art and my aunt Eleanor. Art left our home and for me it was a loss. I missed his humor and wit. One needs that to cover up the daily miseries— just laugh them off, and cover them with humor. Wayne moved to Art's room and I had the loft to myself for a short time, for the move was pending. That move would change my life radically.

Wayne and Cres went looking for a home. They drove all over and finally followed an ad in the paper to a house way out on Sherman Avenue. It was a two-story with an open back porch and an upstairs back porch completely enclosed with screens and windows. The move took place just after school closed. I left all my friends, for this house was a good three miles from North Broom Street. We spent much time cleaning the house. I made the rounds and said goodbyes to my buddies. There would be no more baseball on the school playgrounds or chasing girls at night.

The move came fast. With a rented truck, lots of carrying and lifting, we were there. The home was a typical two-story with a living room, dining room, kitchen, large entrance way with stairs to second floor and a coat closet. There was a half-bath on the first floor. The second floor had a full bath and four bedrooms.

One of those bedrooms was very small. Arrangements were made: Dad and Mom in the large front bedroom, Wayne in the small bedroom next to them, Mary and Cres in the medium-sized back bedroom and I in the back medium-sized bedroom off the porch. It seemed okay then.

The best feature of this house was the lake; it was behind the houses and across the street. Sherman Avenue was a prestigious street. All the houses on the lakeside were pretentious, with lots of backyard down to the lake, and really neat. Our side of the street was for moderate living and homes of ordinary value.

Only one block down from our location was the great city park. It was gorgeous, covering a vast area of, say, four city blocks. It had all the goodies necessary for a park: playgrounds, beach, bathhouse, fishing area, a small wooded area, a river area which ran clear through the city to the other large lake, and a lagoon which ran through the park itself. I loved swimming, so my summer was set for that sport.

The one thing I did not have and did not connect with at that home were playmates of my age. They just were not present. There were a few kids from high school in the area but they were girls and one boy from my grade school but he was not my friend because he was one of the wealthy ones. So I made do and found a school buddy about five blocks away. He had a paper route and asked me if I would take over the route. I talked to my mom and dad and they had no objection. He would hold it through the summer but when winter came he had another job lined up. I went with him at least once a week for a month and then set a date to take over. He went with me to the main office uptown and I signed up, received information about collections and turn-ins, etc. So when school started I would be in business.

The summer was beautiful. I used that gorgeous beach almost every day, swimming out to the small dock. This was a great city beach and very busy on weekends, which I usually avoided because too many families with all their problems populated the area. Usually we were busy taking a drive.

Right after we arrived on Sherman Avenue, I experienced terrible toothaches. I had never been to a dentist, but Mom and the girls had, so I went to their dentist. He said I had terrible tooth problems and needed immediate attention. I had twenty-eight cavities and he immediately pulled one of my teeth out that could not be saved. My mom talked to him and had a cost established. From what I heard she could not pay that amount. He told her he would do it for free if I would work for him and work it off at a dollar for every hour spent on his property. This was agreed to and he proceeded to fix my teeth on weekly visits. His office was very close to our North Broom rental on State Street. So I ventured forth to that sad part of my life with twenty-eight fillings. He used the new stuff called laughing gas and it worked—sometimes. Other times he injected painkiller. It was the ugliest time I can remember except for one period some time later. So I started to work on his property, a lovely lakefront home just down Sherman Avenue about six blocks. I cleaned the lakefront of all the driftwood, dead fish, lake weeds, scum, you name it, around his dock and boat to get it all spiffy clean. In his garage there was a tablet on which I would mark off a dollar an hour. This was the method I worked to pay for the work done on my teeth. He truly was a good man and I thank him to this day for saving my teeth.

I rarely saw his family. One Saturday I was working in the yard, which was large, about 150 feet to the road and from the house to the lake another 100 feet, with lots of trees and growth, bushes of all kinds, and shrubs. He was cutting branches from a tree with his friend. He hollered to me, "Say, John, go to the garage and get the skyhook." I went to the garage and looked for the skyhook and then realized I had been snookered. They had the last laugh on that one.

Between work, swimming, and fishing off the levy, the summer came to an end. My sophomore year and new job would begin.

Going to school from Sherman Avenue was something else. In good weather I could run the two miles in about twenty-five minutes, which I did most of the time. However in bad weather the bus was two blocks away. Sophomore year would be an awakening for me. I carried my lunch and with my grade school buddy, Billy, would go to the Capitol Park on good days and eat on the park benches outside. In bad weather we would go into the Capitol and eat on the many chairs around the halls, looking up at all the beautiful murals, talking, and eating. Dad worked there and he would come by and say hello. At least he was working and happy. They had beautiful restrooms of all marble, clean as a pin. Dad did the plumbing and told me how meticulous they were in keeping everything clean and neat for the legislators and the visiting public. Many people came to see the Capitol since it was really one of a kind, sort of a replica of the national capitol.

So I took over the paper route of ninety-three customers, every day and Sunday, so I began and I did great. It meant getting down to the pick-up area right away after school, half-way to home. The entire route ran about seven blocks long and five blocks wide. That is a lot of area. I would run the route throwing the papers, stopping, folding a bunch, and taking off again. I left my schoolbooks at the store where the pick up began. If you wish to learn responsibility, just become a paperboy. Saturday was collection day, with ninety-three stops most of the time, and I had a few who paid monthly. I would collect the money, take it to the newspaper in the afternoon, pay up, and then have time for myself. Pay off was uptown. I did good in those days—five cents a customer—so I had about five bucks a week for working every day for about fourteen hours a week. With those five bucks I gave my mother two bucks which was a lot in those days. Movies were fifteen to twenty-five cents, candy a nickel, and drinks, too. I saved two to three bucks a week.

I had interesting incidents on that route with drunks; crazy people; mean, kind, and generous people; it ran the entire range of human personality. The greatest time to know people was collection day. My book was accurate and their payments were well recorded. Ninety percent of my ninety-three customers were A+ in payment and kindness. Remember, rain or shine, every day that paper was to be there at that door. Well, the other ten percent ranged from scum to downright stupid. The major problem was getting them to pay *now*, when I arrived. Many times I had to spend other days and evenings collecting the thirty-five cents. With all the problems, work, and frustration it was a rewarding experience.

You talk about people—one day while in the poor neighborhood on my route, one of my older customers was standing looking between two flats. He saw me and said, "Look at those kids." I recognized two of my customer's children. They were about ten to eleven years old, having what appeared to be consensual sex. The old man said, "Hell their parents just do not give a damn." My route was, I believe, a magnifying glass on all mankind. What goes around comes around. You just have to get a set up on living before you start the long voyage called life. Easy for the wealthy, for when they fail it is stupidity, but when the poor fail it is a judgment on society.

While carrying the papers I could see the football team practicing in the large field adjacent to my route. As soon as I finished my route I would run down to the field next to the team and play sandlot football with some friends from high school. One of those friends was Jimmy, I really liked him. One day while he was running from the kickoff, instead of tackling him I tripped him. Boy, he was so mad at me and I was ashamed of myself—why did I do that? That bothered me for a long time although it was just a momentary lack of discipline. I never did it again. In 1942 that good friend would leave school under a deferment to join the marines. He came to me and said, "You can get an immediate diploma if you get your parents to sign for you." Mine would not sign. My good friend the fighting marine was dead a few years later on the shores of Tarawa, an island far from our school. That incident affected me seriously and still does. I consider him a hero, a real man, the reason we all can now live on in a peaceful America.

I was in a typing class as a sophomore, and the football coach knew my eyes were bad, but questioned me on why I could not see the board. I told him the history of my eyes. The other reason he talked to me was to get me on the football team, but I told him my folks had said no. Well he called my folks and insisted they get me glasses and reported it to the school nurse.

Well, miracles never cease—with my sister's money I was sent to an oculist. My eyes read 20/200 and 20/400, according to the oculist, not too far from legally blind without glasses. That was a bit off the wall. He was astounded that I had made it so far in school without glasses, saying I was lucky.

I received the glasses a week later and was actually astounded at what I had been missing. The whole world came to life! It was beautiful—the colors, the textures, the features. The whole world opened up. In school I could see everything. It was wonderful. Then disaster struck—I was leaving school and one of the noisy mean creatures called to me as I was leaving school going down the stairway. He called, "There goes four eyes." I became enraged and attacked with a frenzy known only by idiots. I hit him and he hit me. Then he grabbed me and in the action knocked my glasses off. They crashed to the floor and one lens broke. Well he saw what he did and took off. I was left to go home to report the loss and then get the lens replaced. My sister paid the debt and the lens was replaced. God bless my dear sister, who has gone to her reward. My sight helped me in every way, but I had to be careful—the lesson had been learned in that rage event: Take the glasses off if you are going to be physically active!

That fall our football team was phenomenal. They became champs over and over again. We celebrated after the games by gathering in the university area and drinking beer. Then came the grand event—the university big homecoming fire at the end of the State Street. It would be next Friday night before the Saturday game. That event we kids would attend and really celebrate.

They had the usual large pile of wood, crates, you name it, gathered on the large open field on university land. The crowd was immense, gathering since early evening. The pile was always lit when it became dark outside, so around 7 P.M. the event started.

The crowd that gathered probably was in the number of 600 to 1000. The mix would usually be 90 percent students and the rest townsfolk, mostly young. Many, many had already been consuming alcohol, beer, wine, you name it, so it was a rowdy, fun-loving, hellbent crowd. The female mix was probably 20 percent. Also, the usual engineer-lawyer confrontation was the same day. Competition abounded.

Darkness descended and the bonfire was lit. It was huge! The university cheerleaders gave vent and everyone shouted and screamed for victory tomorrow. It went on and on with people coming and going; going to get more drinks, food, friends, you name it. The crowd grew and grew. My friends and I just enjoyed the whole affair. We had been drinking beer, too and felt really good. As time went on the engineers and lawyers became active in their annual challenge. Some fights started, then the crowd boiled into the State Street and gangs started up State Street toward the capitol, shouting and screaming, then someone was pushed and a store window shattered. From that point windows were broken and goods were stolen. It was still not too late to stop it but the police took time to arrive on the scene. When they did the crowd went crazy. The drinks took over and those who were wound up tight gave vent, shouting, screaming, and breaking more windows. I saw the police cars arrive and the police came out swinging. Near me, two students who had been throwing stones were caught. One large police officer knocked one of them to the ground and tried to put him into the car, but the guy started fighting to get away and the officer used his nightstick on that guy's head twice. Into the car he went. My buddies and I were pressed hard against a store wall; those pressed against glass shattered the glass with their bodies from the pressure. Some people grabbed what they could from the store displays and fled, screaming and shouting. Then the rotten eggs mixed with tear gas were all flying. Wow, what a mess. The crowd dispersed and my friends and I made it up a side street.

I arrived home about 12:30 A.M. filled with the emotion of the evening. How do you really control violence in those situations? How far can police go to control crime or violence or stupidity? It was a good lesson for me. I was like a bystander and had not committed any crime. I did not intend to do any harm, and I was not a drunken and disorderly teen, just a fellow in the crowd. The riot received a lot of national attention. The university published new guides for homecomings. The event had occurred on Saturday night. The next morning I walked to church and crossed the State Street, which showed the chaotic results of the previous night. The streets were littered with paper, broken glass, and debris of all sorts. The smell was atrocious and foul—rotten eggs, tear gas, and other gross smells. The city was furious at inheriting the mess. Changes were in order. The next month, *Life Magazine* featured the event in full color, which put national attention on our university. Broken windows, theft, and destroyed property all made the news, including the arrests and students injured. The following bonfires mellowed into more shouting and screaming for victory than the previous years. It was still fun to go to; in fact we teens standing at the fire were invited to the frat houses to celebrate. They would have washtubs full of beer and of course added the appropriate bottled booze to the mess, then use their cups to become gay and happy. Having been exposed to beer and liquor all my life at home, I knew, as did my friends, what that can do to you. We would have a cup of the mix and that was enough. They ruined the taste of Wisconsin beer with more mix. None of my friends drank to get drunk, it was to be sociable and have a good time. We saw plenty of idiots who did get inebriated, throwing up all over themselves and lying zonked out in the street, but not us.

Christmas came and was better this year since everyone was working. Wayne and Cres decided to get married in the spring. I figured they would move into their own home and there would be changes in my home life. There were more presents and clothes. Cres and Mary bought a new combination radio and phonograph with a nice supply of records. There was lots of dancing around the front room. There was no carpet since the house had wood floors, which had been well kept. Mary had a boyfriend. Howie was a real nice guy and I liked him immediately. His mother had died of cancer and his brother and father lived in Milwaukee. Howie and Mary were meant for each other, as were Cres and Wayne, no doubt about it. They looked and acted like lifelong mates. So there was lots of talk about marriage and all that stuff you know will happen when children marry and leave the nest.

Right after Christmas I developed a sore tooth. It became so sore by the day before New Year that I was in a state of extreme pain. We called the dentist but he was not available till the following Monday. It was a tooth he had filled. The pain was so intense I stayed in bed with packs on my gum. Nothing made the pain subside. I was completely bedridden until Monday, then had to take a bus to the dentist's office downtown. He gave me Novocain, however he drilled into the nerve. The pain was so bad I nearly fainted; he apologized all over the place. When he drilled into the nerve the smell was terrible. There was a cavity behind the filling which caused the intense pain due to pressure from the corruption. In all my life I have had three intense pains: that tooth, the terrible fall in high school that damaged my neck, and a slipped disk on duty in the army, which caused excruciating back pain. Needless to say we are vulnerable and I am fortunate these were not life threatening.

My sophomore year passed quickly, it seemed. My grades were better than average and I became a candidate for junior and turned sixteen as the school year ended. I still hung around with my old friends from other neighborhoods. Billy was my one friend from grade school and high school whom I always made an effort to be with. We had decided to visit the university buildings and look around. Of intense interest was the medical building where they had the cadavers. Billy's brother had attended the university and had told him all about the building. We chose a Saturday and after enjoying the sights on Main Street and around the Capitol Square, we made our way to the old historical building at the university used for medical teaching. Many of the buildings were really old, with architecture reminiscent of bygone days. This building was made of red brick and cement pillars. The door was open, and we saw no one. Billy's brother had told him to go upstairs, which we did.

There was a large open area to our right with all the unique equipment for dissection. There we found a cadaver lying on an open metal table, completely naked. It was a man who appeared to be about fifty-five at death. Parts of his arms and his lower legs were under dissection.

As grotesque as it appeared, it was fascinating. The smell of that carcass was overwhelming. He had turned color and was sort of dark brown. We figured the embalming solution was the weird smell. What a scene, and he was the only one there. There was nothing else to be seen except the tables for student use.

Billy's brother had told him there was a chute from the embalming floor down to the ground in case of fire. Great—where was it? We searched and found the entrance door and it opened easily. The entrance was to a large circular tube that wound down and we could see the first ten to twelve feet and then nothing. Billy said, "Let's go," and we did. What a ride! Down and down, circle after circle, then light and we shot out onto the grass. Later I thought what if there had been a door at the end, but we figured, no, that would defeat escape. Well, it was exciting.

We had heard of another building that housed the biological exhibits from years past. Billy had an idea of its location, so we went there. It was a smaller building, newer and more modern. The door was open and we could hear talking down the hall. Billy said the exhibits were in the basement so down we went. I had never seen such a bunch of creations. Rooms with jars, rooms with stuffed animals, birds, and small critters. The jars held snakes, entrails, various strange-looking bugs and worms, on and on. There were stuffed birds of all types dated from years before. We figured they were dated so that changes could be detected over time. There were all sorts of things, butterflies and bugs, you name it. We spent a great deal of time there and left feeling that some students spent a lot of time hunting critters of all sorts.

Our visit to the campus was completed so we walked down to the State Street and noticed the military recruiting display in a store close to the campus for army, navy, and marine. The recruiters were not there but the information was so we looked it over. War was a prospect for America, with lots to talk about our entrance in the battle due to England's tenuous situation and Hitler's indifference to world pleas. I looked at the navy displays and Billy looked at air force displays. Both of us had bad eyes and wondered about our future if we did go to war.

The summer was one of work and play. My paper route was my moneymaker, with swimming at the nearby beach and fishing as my great companions. I liked to fish alone and I usually caught bass and perch off the rocks at the park early in the morning. Once the beach house was open, the crowds came. The rocks I fished off of were at the end of the beach and it became too noisy by 10 A.M., so I fished early.

Living near the lake each year produced drowning. It is a sad state of affairs, but people are careless. They drink and swim, go too far out, and are not trained to survive in water, or they go when they should not because they are sick, tired, drunk, whatever. Water is dangerous. Boating accidents also caused death. That summer a home across the street provided a death. I went over as the fire rescue team came. They dragged the young girl from the water but it was too late. What a waste. That summer I watched the boats dragging for a body that went down about a week before. They finally snagged the body and brought it in to shore. I stood looking down at what was a middle-aged man, blue and bloated—ghastly. It pays to be careful.

We never had a boat and as I said previously, my dad never did own a car, only had driven the old Model T truck, so I had no real incentive to own a vehicle. Wayne brought that to our home. He also brought the ability to rent boats and fish, which I did with him and Dad on two occasions. One time when we were fishing from the boat near shore, say about 150 feet from shore, we had not caught any fish. I was looking over the side and could not believe what I saw—a fish almost four feet long. Wayne and Dad looked too. It was a large old fish; I had no idea what kind. It looked like a huge pike, but did they get that big? Wayne said it looked like a garpike or pike of some sort. It was huge. No wonder the fish didn't bite. That fish moved slowly away. We fished with night crawlers but nothing that fish would bite on. As it does on those lakes, the wind came up and with it the waves increased in size till the boat was rocking back and forth, taking in water. Luckily we were near land, so Dad and I rowed into shore and got out. The boat, with Wayne at the oars, was about three city blocks from the pier. We watched him row in the swells back to the dock where we met him, and he was really worn out.

One evening my mother went out to the clothesline to bring in the dried clothes. We were all in the kitchen with the girls making supper and Dad was just home from work. We heard Mom scream and looking out, saw her dancing an Irish jig, up and down and all around, screaming, "It is getting me!" She ran into the kitchen and kept pulling up her long dress, dancing around, higher and higher, as she screamed, "Get it off me!" Well, Dad came to the rescue. He grabbed her and she danced close to him and he pulled up her dress to her neck. Wow—we never had seen our mom's underclothes on her and it was a sight. There was a huge miller moth, at least that was what Dad called it. They are about the size of a bat. It flew to the ceiling and she dropped to the floor with his help. What a scene! It took forever it seemed to get the moth and put its remains outside. Mom was really mad because we laughed so hard, some of us, including me, were rolling on the floor.

One other event: I had been doing a lot of reading on Marconi and other inventors. Wayne had an old crystal set that we had used on North Broom Street to hear a station at night. Well I figured I might get more stations out of it than just one. Being inexperienced in the effects of electricity, without much forethought I took a plug-in wire and cut the other end off, then put the crystal set on one of our kitchen tables, and cleaned the ends of the cord. Then the fun began. I plugged in the cord, touched the crystal set in two places, and WOW! The sparks flew, my fingers burned, all the lights in the kitchen and other places went out, and of course the crystal set was a melted mess. Learning is hard and also so painful to one's ego. I did not hear the end of that one for a long time.

Wayne and Cres's marriage had been delayed to midsummer. There was a lot of preparation. He had bought her an engagement ring and now had selected the wedding ring. Mother was in a dither. She was the first child to leave the nest, or was she. We would find out soon. The wedding would be at the old church we still attended, now by car, bus, or walking (rarely), near downtown.

I was an usher along with several of Wayne's friends. His job at the post office as a clerk was his main topic of conversation. He was absolutely consumed by the job and loved it. He had found his niche. I was told that he was excellent at casing mail, the fastest and most accurate. He was proud of his work and as a very intelligent adult, was meticulous in his work; whatever he did, he did well.

The wedding was exciting. The whole family on Grandmother's side attended along with several of Wayne's new friends at the post office. They were exceedingly happy and the day was one of great success. A beautiful summer day, just perfect.

They went on their honeymoon; it would be for a week. Off they went. Now I was not aware of any prior discussions on what would occur after the wedding. The "what after" must have been planned with my mother for some time. They came home and it was now known that they would live with my mother and dad forever. I say that now because that is what happened. The front bedroom was too small for them so they took my room and I went to the porch. The problem with that was I could hear them in their room. Obviously the house was poorly insulated and the large bedroom window looked out on the porch, which was a poor arrangement. So there we were, right back to as it was, except that now they slept together. I was disturbed by this event but what could I do? Live with it, kid, it ain't going to change.

Something strange happened. My sister Mary bought me a bike. I had never had a two-wheeler, although Uncle Art had taught me to ride on one when we lived on North Broom. One of the days he was teaching me I slammed into a barn door and injured my knee. What pain I had for a long time. Art was so good to me.

Well, that bike became a time saver for me getting to school and back and getting me home from the paper route, too.

School began. I was sixteen, a junior, and with my new glasses I could see and had for all summer. Things were so bright and interesting. I used the bike in good weather for school. That year I took auto mechanics and drafting, both were hands-on courses and I liked them. I received an A+ in auto mechanics and a B in drafting. My other courses were Bs and Cs. I loved history and had great history teachers; I loved to read and enjoyed the English literature. We read *Jane Eyre* and many English poems. It was an interesting year for selecting novels and writing reports.

Noon hours Billy and I ate together in summer on the benches at the Capitol Park and in rainy or cold weather we ate in the Capitol building itself. It was interesting and we enjoyed the beauty and the clean restrooms. Lots of kids ate there and some stayed at school and ate in the lunchroom. If we had spare time we would look in the stores and do our wishing.

The games were great and again we enjoyed them. I had found some good friends in my neighborhood on the paper route from school so I went to games with them. We also played ball on weekends and after school, for me it was after the paper route. Our school had several plays, which I always enjoyed. I never participated but enjoyed watching others perform. I wished my personality had been more outgoing but it was not. I believe the treatment I received in grade school set me back, at least that is my recollection of the reason. One has to be given support in some of those more courageous decisions. I always felt left out. If that is a good explanation, it seems so.

Wayne, Cres, Mary, and Howie did many things together. They would go down to Chicago on weekends to dance at the Avalon or Trianon ballroom where the best big bands played. This was at least a once-a-month event. Howie worked at the same state agency as Mary and Cres. They were all employed and doing well. Dad and Mom were all right with Cres and Wayne assisting in food and rent. I decided that with the war building, if the need came, I would be gone.

We did not go to Grandmother's that often since we were so far away and the activity with more adults around kept us busy, especially Mom. She insisted on doing the wash, ironing, cooking, and house cleaning. That was her mistake. With the responsibility growing, it became apparent that there was more work. This responsibility she accepted but by the same token expected that she would get what she wanted. What Mom wanted was trips in the car, rides in the country, etc. In other words, she wanted to have some excitement in her life. Those facts tended to put tension in the lives of the married or soon-to-be-married couples. It was evident that Mary and Howie would marry soon, but when.

During the late fall Wayne became seriously ill. His health grew worse and worse. Soon the doctor decided that this guy was eligible to be hospitalized. The doctors at St. Mary's hospital found he had a case of pneumonia so severe that they put drains in his lungs. Mother would make almost daily trips on the bus to see him. If I was home she took me, too. His condition worsened, and the priest said the last rites. This was the time that the new sulfa drugs were popular and had been doing miracles with infections. They started to administer sulfa by mouth to Wayne. Gradually he improved, however it was necessary to operate and remove a portion of his rib cage. This improved the drainage from the immense infection. It was the putrid green slime in the drainage bag. It was awful. For me, I enjoyed the cafeteria at the hospital. They had the best ham sandwiches, lemon pie, and milk and you could get all for thirty cents. He was hospitalized for a month and then came home. Mom put him in the small front bedroom, and I could not believe his body—you could feel all his ribs, his arms were just long bones, and he looked like a living skeleton. He recovered slowly and it was late in January before he saw work again. Once he started on the road to recovery, it was swift.

Our Christmas had been bleak with Wayne ill, but we had some good meals and got by in fine shape. I took the bus to work quite often that winter because the streets were really icy and I could not ride my bike.

School was going fine. My friends and I attended all the basketball games. Our team was terrific and we had one good time. After the games we would walk downtown and enjoy the company of the university gang, just a bit older but fun to watch. None of us had girlfriends; it was much different then now days. We visited with girls and enjoyed their company but dating cost too much.

My grades were good not great. I still had the paper route but was looking around for something else to make money with and found a job through a friend at the uptown drugstore; a chain drugstore owned by the state's governor. He owned the local chain. They were Rexall Drugstores. The job was as a dishwasher and the pay was twenty-five cents an hour. My hours were Saturday night and Sunday morning. My responsibility was wash dishes on Saturday, start at 4 P.M., close up the store at 12 A.M., open Sunday morning at 6 A.M., work washing dishes and starting coffee and work until 1 P.M. it sounded good so I accepted the job to start February 1.

I had a fellow take over the route and walked it with him three times then signed off. The job at the drugstore was a real load. The combination drugstore and food counter was one load of work. Being right uptown, one block from the Capitol, meant lots of business. There were two major theaters on the same block and on weekends students flocked to the evening movies. I washed dishes until I just about concluded this job must end. Well, the counterman a student who did all the loading of the long ice cream counters, emptied the garbage, generally instructed the new counter employees, and served customers at the counter and the many tables. Carrying out a garbage can full of liquid, etc., he developed a hernia. This happened a month after I started. The drugstore manager came by and said, "You can support the counter and I will get a new dishwasher," which he did. From then on for the next four months I did that job and it was not bad.

At home Mary and Howie decided to get married and it would be a quiet affair in April, real soon. The wedding in the rectory of the church, was beautiful. Mary was dressed in a blue velvet suit and looked beautiful. They went on a short honeymoon.

CHAPTER 9:

1942: Gorham Street, Sixteen to Eighteen—Oh Salvation, Oh War

When they returned a week later they were put to moving into an apart-ment just two blocks away. We helped them move some things from our house and saw them settled in. They were very happy and I missed Mary immediately. Wayne and Cres went looking for another house for the two families. They found one two blocks away, very close to where Mary and Howie were living. The house had a large lot with a two-car garage, three good-sized bedrooms, one with an area for a baby bed that was separate. There was a bath on the second floor and a half-bath on the first floor. Well, that was it for me. Move, move, move; that was my life, however it was a lit-tle closer to school. My last school year was approaching and then would come decisions.

Before we moved, I was injured. While I opened a large refrigerator door, another employee slammed the door shut on my right index finger. It was hanging and bleeding with a large split near the first joint. So much blood spurted out that I laid down on the floor. The manager on the drugstore side came over and for no good reason cursed me as though it was my fault; it was not. It was terribly busy, at about 11 P.M. He was a drugo; I saw him drinking Coke syrup out of the big barrels in the basement like water. Well, that fin-ished me. I was sent to the hospital, given shots, and it was stitched up. One week later my arm began to swell while I was at a movie on Sunday afternoon. I went home and the swelling continued all over my body, although it had started at the point of the shot entrance. I was driven to the hospital and they said I had a reaction to the tetanus. Now my aunt, the nurse, told my moth-er she had the same reaction once and it can be fatal if you get the shot again. However, once was enough. My whole body swelled up, then after twenty-four hours it turned fire red and burned, then it changed to pain in all the

99

joints, which lasted another twenty-four hours, followed by shedding skin all over my body. I was out of school for about nine days. During the bad time I was taken to the hospital and was given a shot in the chest, but what it was I do not know. I was sent home and from then on I started to recover.

I quit the job and filed a report. Our move took place around Easter time. I was given a small bedroom in the back of the second floor; it was okay. Wayne and Cres had the large front bedroom and Dad and Mom in the middle. I guess they were figuring on starting a family and would need the crib area.

There was a small Kroger store at the corner and the manager asked me if I wanted to work there at fifty cents an hour. I said great and started. I fixed the vegetable area, swept the floor, stacked shelves, and worked the counter. It was great. I worked there weekends and some evenings. However, after about three weeks I developed a peeling of skin from my hands. I showed the school nurse my hands and she asked what I did. I told her and she thought it was an allergic reaction to the vegetables. Well, as I now look back, I should have told her about the allergic attack because of the tetanus shot. Anyway, I lost the job, darn it. I really liked that position.

I was busy the rest of spring getting caught up at school, I had lost weight and was feeling weak and was generally not well. I passed my junior year and at the ripe age of seventeen in 1941, I was ready for my senior year in high school.

The war was churning on and there was great worry over our entrance. Would we fight the Nazis, what would we do for England, and how could they exist with the constant bombing of their cities, especially London? There was tension in the air. The new rental was okay but not especially satisfying. It looked good from the outside but for living it was not that livable. I knew Mom was not satisfied. She did a lot of complaining about the house and I didn't blame her. She missed her rides, which had more or less stopped because of Wayne's work schedule. He was working nights and days on differing schedules, weekends too. She still did all the work. Dad and Wayne did wash walls, painting, fixing faucets, doors, etc. Well, we got by. There was less or no fishing and very few rides. Dad didn't drive, nor did either of the girls or me. I had my bike and had to take Wayne's lunch to him in a lunch box periodically. He never knew if there would be a need to work overtime.

On one of the return trips on my bike I rounded a corner in front of the train station. A driver opened his door as I passed his car and my bike struck the open door. I cartwheeled over the door with pain in my whole body. My knee was cut and my new bike was damaged. The driver started hollering and cursing me. If I had known then that a driver is at blame when he opens the door into traffic, I would have called a cop. Anyway, I walked the bike home, had to buy a new wheel, and lived with a damaged bike. It seemed the world just dealt me bad blows. Why me?

My senior year began and it was interesting. I was an average student, our football and basketball teams were tops in the state, and Cres was pregnant. Now it seemed to me that they would live with Dad and Mom forever. That is actually how it all developed for the next thirty-five years together as married people. Was it good, bad? Who knows. It would not be for me, as I was too independent. However, Mom and Dad did help to raise Cres's four children, sharing everything. So be it.

Well, I had heard about jobs being available at the large Oscar Mayer meat packing plant in town, so I put my name in. They promised me a job at graduation. So I was set on that. Meantime Wayne gave me driving lessons so there would be another driver. It took me two times but I did it. The guy who tested me, as he did with everyone, made you stop on a street with a grade that seemed to be vertical, stop, then shift on the hill without sliding back. Well, I did it the second time.

Wayne had traded the Buick for a Nash, which drove very well. It was a nice riding car. The school year went very well. On December 7 I was at a movie theater uptown when I heard this hollering outside. It was the man who sold papers around the Capitol, a nice older man. I heard him say as he always did if there was a real story, "Wuxtra, Wuxtra, read all about it, Japs attack Pearl Harbor." He must have been in the lobby. I left and saw the headlines. I started to run home, tears running down my cheeks. I was mad, mad, and was going to enlist. That locked-in Hun was ready for battle.

At home it was shock. The radio blurted out the horrible news; we had lost the Pacific fleet except for some carriers and some ships. However, it was a disaster. We listened to the president the next day as he addressed the nation. Everyone slept with worried minds that night. Wayne and Howie talked of being sent.

The next day at school we were all assembled in the auditorium for the president's address. Also on the stage was a large screen about five feet by four feet. The first thing that happened was the president spoke on the situation as it stood. He was declaring war on Japan, and the declaration on Germany came later. The speech also indicated conscription was now being installed. Also, the screens were something called television, experimental, but it did show pictures being sent from one part of the auditorium to another. The word was it was someday going to be in all homes.

This started a lot of worrying in the family. Would the two men be sent to duty? We guys at school got all the info. The feeling of security for the family was disrupted. Our family unit was now just recovering from the Depression, not entirely, but much better than it had been. Now if the two men left, how would the rest survive? Military pay was not that much for a private. It appeared we would again have money worries. Our radio constantly ground out bad news. There seemed no end in sight. Wayne and Howie were all excited about their futures in the military. Wayne was sure they would end up in postal units. In fact a recruiter had told them that at their age, married and with postal training, that was a good option. I was skeptical since everyone I knew who went in ended up in the infantry.

The rest of the year was spent in war, war, and war. I graduated and became eighteen. I was registered for war and waited. We celebrated our graduation. Billy had his dad's Buick, so we asked girls to go and they said yes. We went to a popular golf club dining room selected by parents and students with our dates, ate, danced, had a glass of wine, and went home. We had completed all the requirements for graduation. I was now eighteen on graduation day and ready for war.

Mobilization was everywhere. They established Truax Field at our local air base and had started shipping in the necessary personnel to get the building accomplished for the many recruits needed for operation of the base. Soon the town was filled with military personnel.

The university established a training program for officers and soon there were officer candidates on the streets. The girls at school were ecstatic. They could get dates with real men now.

I started working at Oscar Mayer as a clerk first in reproduction and finally in writing checks at the stockyard. It was from that job I left for service in the army in January 1943. My buddies Billy and John and I went to the various recruiting stations. We were told with our eyes as bad as they were we would only be qualified for the army. Billy ended up in army engineering, John ended up in air force photography, and I ended up in the army in the coast artillery. My number for call up would be in middle '43; I decided to go after Christmas 1943. I would be eighteen and a half. Wayne and Howie were both called and both were 4F. The wives were glad; they were not. Wayne's lungs were too bad and Howie's eyes were much worse than mine. I worked through the year at eighteen dollars a week. I saved money, paid money to my mom, and got ready to leave. The war was going to be long and costly; flags were in the windows, some gold for a death in the family, and you could see them on the streets. We all prepared to go with lots of thought on the good-byes. On January 29, 1943, I had my physical, refused a two week leave, and found myself the next morning at a naval station in Chicago called Sheridan, used for briefing recruits, shots, etc., and assignment to duty. I was in the army with no regrets. I shed no tears. I was prepared to do my best for God and country. What else could the nation expect in time of war? What happened to me in the following years and my family is another story.

I had lived through the Depression in several ways. I felt no longer depressed.

What went through my mind were the incidents related in this book. Was it the mistreatment in grade school, a lack of concern at home for my physical well being, or the course of events as they unfolded during those early years from birth to eighteen? The lack of wealth certainly played a definitive role in all the events as they unfolded. We were fortunate to survive as well as we did and now I thank God for having provided the many experiences, for they were rare, amusing, and educational. Our families did all right. The war provided myself with the growth and maturity necessary and provided at just the right time, it was my childhood dream to be a soldier and so it became real. What more can anyone hope for, a dream, wish, and desire fulfilled.

My Catholic education did not end in grade school. Although high school was not parochial, it was another great event in my life. I was propelled from a very regimented environment into a structured education system, allowing one to progress through different instructors skilled in several subjects. Also, the change in students during the day allowed more social growth. The students were also from different cultures, races, and with ethnic backgrounds, which fashioned new conversations and knowledge. I was truly happy.

My college education after the war was in schools affiliated with religious institutions. There were lay teachers and religious teachers who were available for certain subjects. Those orders made sure that the students were well qualified in their chosen studies. A Catholic education provided in the 1920s and 1930s was far different, depending on nuns and priests to do all the educating.

The religious orders of nuns in those days were assigned to schools to provide religious instruction and necessary education required by state certification. Those nuns were not paid employees; their funds came from several sources, some from the orders, some from the parish contributions made at religious masses, individual wealthy contributors, and the families of the nuns and priests assigned to the parish. So it was that the children of wealthy contributors received recognition beyond that of the poor givers. It was not right, but who knows, we see the same in everyday life, in politics especially so. However right or wrong, it did affect my sisters and my life in those early days of the Depression. Those days were dark for the poor. We were victims since our parents were in desperate straits.

Years earlier when we used to visit my aunts who were nuns and even superiors of nuns in various Wisconsin cities, they would tell my mother, "Elsie, you have no idea how difficult it is to manage the women assigned to those schools. They are human beings with the same problems you find just about anywhere."

I agree we cannot set nuns and priests on pedestals. They are only human. Idolizing the religious is not only improper, but it is immoral. They are God's workers on earth in their chosen profession, doing what every Christian is prescribed to do by God.

Some priests are assigned to run parishes and schools. Their job is enormous, running the circle of paying off mortgages to new building programs to instituting changes directed from on high, and of course running the day-to-day activities necessary for all Christians.

Priests and nuns are married to God and that is fact. They cannot again be married unless they leave the church, although in the past few years because of the lack of interest in the priesthood, the church has enlisted some help. I have been told married priests from non-Catholic orders have been accepted into the Catholic faith as priests with one stipulation: If your wife dies you are not allowed to remarry. Also, married deacons have been ordained priests with the same stipulation, and why not. Our great savior God forgives all, even those priests who have given up their marriage to Him, forsaking their vows, performing hideous acts and perversions of all kinds. Our God will forgive if they truly repent their transgressions.

I believe someday the priests and nuns will be allowed to marry, have families, and serve their parishes, schools, communities, and our great savior, God. That change will save the Catholic faith and fulfill God's grand design for all mankind on earth. Perhaps priests who would marry would not be allowed to become bishops, archbishops, cardinals, etc. They would remain priests in their particular order. Celibate priests would be eligible to move up the ladder in their orders. That sounds fair.

AFTERWORD

These memories do not justify, crucify, or castigate any one person. They are what happened at a point in time. What one does as interaction during life reflects in many ways the essence of being. Character develops from those interactions. Each person develops their character for better or worse based on those occurrences.

I was prepared to kill those who threatened my country. To die, in my mind, meant eternal salvation, as told, to be with God instantly. That is what we were told. Is it not all the same, are not all on the same level? Each religion has that dream of eternal salvation and reward. Far better that we all just accept the fact that dying is eternal. When one goes fishing, they satisfy a desire; when one dies, eternal peace is forever. God is God for all, Moslem, Jew, Buddhist, Christian, and all others.

So, looking back, nearing the end of my life, I find only joy in living this long, being moderately successful in all I have accomplished. Only God can be the judge of how one person's character fulfilled the reason for living and, He is all forgiving, for we are all only human. These are my opinions based on my life working in many fields of military and civilian occupations.

Peace and Love,
John Joseph Daniels

ABOUT THE AUTHOR

Having lived through the deep Depression of the 1920s and 1930s, John J. Daniels made a life of military and government service. His education following WWII was at the University of Wisconsin, Madison; University of Wisconsin, Milwaukee; then transferred to the University of Albuquerque, achieving a bachelor of university studies (cum laude), and a master's of science in hospital administration from Cardinal Stritch College, now a university in Milwaukee, Wisconsin. He graduated from the Brooke Army Medical Center, San Antonio, Texas, from the medical associate army officer career course. He served in the United States Army from 1943-1946, joining the United States Army Reserve upon discharge. He attained the rank of chief warrant officer 4 (CWO4) and was discharged July 1, 1984 at sixty years of age. He worked as a metal spinner for a short period of time after WWII then for the U.S. Postal Service. In 1962 he was selected by the Veterans Administration and rose to the personnel officer level, traveling through many Veterans Administration hospitals and their Washington, D.C., central office.

The United States Navy hired him at the naval air station located in Bermuda for three years as the director of civilian personnel. He retired form federal service in July 1984.

His civilian and military service took him from Wisconsin, to Georgia, Florida, New York, Long Island, Okinawa, Washington State, California, New Mexico, Washington D.C., Texas, Virginia, Bermuda, North Carolina, and England, not quite in that order, but he was assigned to a couple locations twice.